Mr. Big

Mr. Big

Exposing Undercover Investigations in Canada

Kouri T. Keenan & Joan Brockman

Fernwood Publishing • Halifax and Winnipeg

Editing: Judith Kearns and Brian Turner
Cover design: John van der Woude
Text design: Brenda Conroy
Printed and bound in Canada by Hignell Book Printing

Mixed Sources
Product group from well-managed
forests and other controlled sources
www.fsc.org Cert no. SW-COC-003438
© 1996 Forest Stewardship Council

Published in Canada by Fernwood Publishing
32 Oceanvista Lane
Black Point, Nova Scotia, B0J 1B0
and 748 Broadway Avenue, Winnipeg, Manitoba, R3G 0X3
www.fernwoodpublishing.ca

Fernwood Publishing Company Limited gratefully acknowledges the financial support of the
Government of Canada through the Canada Book Fund, the Canada Council for the Arts,
the Nova Scotia Department of Tourism and Culture and the Province of Manitoba,
through the Book Publishing Tax Credit, for our publishing program.

Library and Archives Canada Cataloguing in Publication

Keenan, Kouri T.
Mr. Big : exposing undercover investigations in
Canada / Kouri T. Keenan and Joan Brockman.

Includes bibliographical references.
ISBN 978-1-55266-376-9

1. Undercover operations—Canada—Case studies. 2. Confession (Law)—Canada—Case studies. 3.
Police questioning—Canada—Case studies. 4. Police—Canada—Case studies. 5. Criminal justice,
Administration of—Canada—Case studies. I. Brockman, Joan II. Title. III. Title: Mister Big.

HV8080.U5K45 2010   363.2'320971   C2010-902727-2

Contents

1

An Introduction to Mr. Big

How do you get sucked in? Well, out here [on a reserve] it's close to poverty. There's no jobs. All you have to do is pick something up here and take it there for $500 to $1000. Who's going to turn that down? Obviously, I didn't (Mentuck quoted in Burns 2009).

... the police must be aware that as the level of inducement increases, the risk of receiving a confession to an offence which one did not commit increases, and the reliability of the confession diminishes correspondingly. In this case, in my view, the level of inducement was overpowering ... it provided nothing but upside for the accused to confess and a downside of frustration and despair in maintaining his denial (Mr. Justice MacInnes in *Mentuck* 2000b: para. 100.)[1]

When people with minor or even extensive criminal pasts, and who appear not to have made much money in their lives, are suddenly befriended and paid increasingly large sums of money for committing crimes in an apparently secure environment, they want such a pattern of life to continue, and indeed, to get even better — that is, more lucrative. Like many other people in society who are motivated by greed and profit, such as some directing and executive officers of large corporations, they will readily cheat and lie to obtain these goals (Nowlin 2004: 395).

One need not be referred to evidence to acknowledge the ubiquitous nature of criminal activity in our society. If the struggle against crime is to be won, the ingenuity of criminals must be matched by that of the police; as crimes become more sophisticated so too must be the methods employed to detect their commission (Mr. Justice Antonio Lamer in *Mack* 1988: para. 15).

Andrew Rose

On October 6, 1983, the bodies of two German travelers were discovered in a wooded area approximately thirty-two kilometres west of Chetwynd, British Columbia. Both victims had been shot in the head (*Rose* 1991: para. 3). The victims' camping gear, passports, and travellers' cheques were missing from the crime scene, suggesting robbery as a motive. The following day, a pair of bloodstained blue jeans, waist size 34 inches, was discovered a few kilometres from the crime scene. A forensic serologist determined that the blood was consistent with that of the victims (*Rose* 1991: para. 6). Alas, the case went cold, and nearly six years passed before the RCMP would catch the break they anxiously needed.

In August 1989, Madonna Mary Kelly, an acquaintance of Andrew Rose, who was then living in Newfoundland, told a drug dealer who was staying with her that on the night of the murders Rose came to her home covered in blood, claiming to have just killed two people. The drug dealer turned out to be an undercover police informant who subsequently relayed the information to the RCMP. As a result, Andrew Rose was arrested and charged with the double murder of the German tourists (*Rose* 1991: para. 8).

Although Rose acknowledged that he wore size 34 jeans in 1983, the prosecution was unable to prove that the bloodstained jeans belonged to him. As Gudjonsson indicates, the circumstantial evidence was in Rose's favour; he did not have access to firearms, he did not cash the travellers' cheques belonging to the victims (the victims' travellers' cheques were cashed by someone other than the accused), and he did not own a vehicle (2003b: 574). Since there was no other evidence linking Rose to the crime, the incriminating statements he made to Madonna Kelly would become the lynchpin in the Crown's case (*Rose* 1991: para. 10). Notwithstanding the lack of physical evidence, Rose was convicted of the murders on the testimony of Kelly. However, in 1992, the British Columbia Court of Appeal overturned the guilty verdict, finding that there was significant circumstantial evidence that could have raised a reasonable doubt about his guilt (*Rose* 1992: para. 45).

At his second trial, Rose was again convicted of the double homicide. Once more, the only evidence connecting him to the murders was the testimony of Madonna Mary Kelly (para. 4). Subsequent to his second trial, Rose provided the RCMP with a blood sample for DNA analysis, which excluded Rose as a source of the DNA found at the crime scene (Gudjonsson 2003b: 575). In addition, the RCMP followed up on a confession made about the murders by one Vance Hill to his estranged wife. Hill's story was consistent with the facts of the case. Unfortunately, Hill committed suicide on July 28, 1985, making it impossible to confirm the veracity of his statements (*Rose* 1998: para. 6). In light of the fresh evidence, Rose was granted yet another trial (Gudjonsson 2003b: 575).

Perhaps because of tunnel vision, Gudjonsson notes, Canadian police were concerned that the newly acquired exculpatory evidence could result in Rose's acquittal. Such tunnel vision then led the RCMP to trick Rose into confessing by engaging him in an undercover operation (2003b: 575). As part of his bail conditions, Rose was required to sign in at the RCMP headquarters in Thompson, Manitoba, where he had taken up residence. Outside the station, he was introduced to UC1,[2] an undercover police officer posing as the main contact for a wealthy criminal organization (Burke 2009). UC1 was charged with the task of befriending Rose, which he did by hiring him to do a job for the criminal syndicate. Over the next few months, UC1 involved Rose in a series of various criminal activities, mainly to do with drug trafficking, for which Rose was paid (Gudjonsson 2003b: 575). UC1 indicated to Rose that he could stand to profit a great deal from the organization but that he would have to meet with UC2, "Mr. Big," to discuss some troubling issues in his past that could jeopardize his career in the organization. UC2 claimed to be able to help him with his problems and the murder charges, stating, "If I fucking help you, you would be guaranteed not to be found guilty.... You won't even go to another trial" (578).

During the undercover interrogation sessions, Rose was subjected to what Gudjonsson would later call "relentless pressure, abusive language, threats, inducements, robust challenges and psychological manipulation" (2003b: 578). He emphatically stated that he could not and would not confess to a crime he did not commit. The following exchange took place between Mr. Big and Rose:

> UC2: Yeah, that's a lie, that's a fuckin' lie right off the bat. Cuz everything I fuckin' found out about it, the evidence is all fuckin' there that you did it. They convicted you twice on the fuckin' thing; they can convict you a third time. Listen, I don't give a fuck.
> Rose: I do not lie to you.
> UC2: I don't give a fuck, let's get that clear. But, if you're just gonna lie to me, and you don't want fuckin' help, then I can't help you. I'm helping you because...
> Rose: If I tell you I didn't do it and you don't believe I didn't do it. What am I supposed to say? I need your help.
> UC2: Yeah, well, you're not gonna fuckin' get it unless I get the fuckin' story. And I'll explain to you how...
> Rose: I didn't do it.
> UC2: I'll explain to you how I can fuckin' help you.
> Rose: What can I say now?
> UC2: Tell me the truth.
> Rose: I didn't do it.
> UC2: Come clean with me and I'll tell you how I'm gonna help you.
> Rose: I didn't do it.
> UC2: Well then you don't need my help.
> Rose: I'll never say I did it. I'll never say I did it, cuz I didn't.
> UC2: Well...
> Rose: So, what can I say?
> UC2: Well, if you didn't do it, you don't need my help. Let's let the fuckin' courts decide. If I fuckin' help you out you'd be guaranteed not to be found guilty, but I'm not fuckin' helping you out for the fuckin' uh, I don't fuckin'...
> Rose: Yeah, but you want me to say I'm guilty.
> UC2: I want the fuckin' uh, I want to be able to fuckin' trust you. When I leave this fuckin' room I know I've got a guy I fuckin' trust.
> Rose: I know...

UC2: All the fuckin' circumstances I have found out and I've looked into I have fuckin' come away fuckin' saying, "Okay, this guy offs these two people, I don't give a fuck why. That's the least of my fuckin' worries. I will help him if he fuckin' just comes clean, and if he doesn't, then I'm not givin' him a fuckin' minute of my fuckin' time anymore".

Rose: I didn't do it, okay?

UC2: Well then, there you go. You don't need my fuckin' help, do you?

Rose: Damn right I do.

UC2: You better come clean.

Rose: Well, I'm still not gonna say I did it, cuz I didn't. So, what am I supposed to say?

UC2: From what I know, you haven't got a chance. That lady from the States, she'll not be givin' the evidence you think she's gonna be givin'.

Rose: No?

UC2: The police have been fuckin' soft-shoein' her big time. That's why this has been fuckin' delayed the way it is. (Burke, 2009)

Despite considerable psychological manipulation and pressure to break down Rose's resistance, persuade him of his guilt, and elicit a confession by reiterating the strength of the evidence against him and the likelihood of a third conviction, Rose repeatedly and emphatically denied any involvement in the double murders.

Rose: I'll tell you right now, if this means the end of me and you and [UC1] whatever… I will not say I did it. That's it. Then I'm outta here, you know, simple as that. That's the way she goes. I will not say I did it when I didn't do it, and I didn't do it and that's it.

UC2: Go downstairs to the lounge, have one fuckin' beer, think this over.

Rose: Well, I'm not gonna come back up here and say I killed them. (Burke 2009)

Following their discussions, Rose and UC1 went downstairs to the lounge where they spent almost two hours drinking beer (Gudjonsson 2003b: 579). Although it is unclear how much alcohol was consumed, Rose's lawyer later commented he was an alcoholic "plied with liquor," and CBC's News' *The Fifth Estate* reporter, Linden MacIntyre, described him as "fortified with beer" (Burke 2009).

After repeated and emphatic denials to Mr. Big, a man who arguably undermined Rose's confidence in both the criminal justice system and his legal team (Burke 2009),[3] Andy Rose would eventually confess, telling UC1 and UC2 what they wanted to hear: "Well, we'll go with I did it, okay?" In the end, RCMP operatives elicited a confession from him in the second and third interrogation sessions, which were audio and videotaped (Burke 2009). Not surprisingly, Rose was unable to provide undercover operators with specific details — outside the scope of those already known to the police or media — about the circumstances surrounding the double murders. For instance, when asked where he got the firearm, he responded, "Oh I had it, I had it" (Gudjonsson 2003b: 579). Rose's numerous attempts to retract his confession would prove futile. When confronted by his sister as to why, after years of denying the murders, he would confess to something he did not do, he said he wanted it to "go away" (Burke 2009). Anyone watching the videotape available through the documentary (Burke 2009) would be hard pressed to conclude Rose was not lying when he "confessed" to the murders.

At Rose's third trial, defence counsel sought to qualify as an expert Dr. Gisli H. Gudjonsson, a professor of forensic psychology at King's College London and a forensic psychologist with special expertise in the area of police interrogation and false confession. It was hoped that Gudjonsson would give evidence about the scientific literature related to false confessions, the nature of police interrogation techniques, the similarities between non-custodial and custodial interrogation techniques, the factors in this case consistent with those typically found in cases of false confessions, the results of the psychological evaluation, and the reliability of Rose's admission to RCMP operatives (Gudjonsson 2003b: 580).

In addition to conducting a psychological evaluation of Rose, Dr. Gudjonsson read through transcripts of the telephone conversations and interviews with undercover officers, listened to audiotape evidence, and watched the videotapes of the interviews with undercover officers. Significantly, as already noted, Gudjonsson (2003b) found evidence of "relentless pressure, abusive language, threats, inducements, robust challenges and psychological manipulation" (578). He concluded that the "immense pressure that Rose was placed under, and the extreme distress he displayed during the three videotaped interviews, raises important ethical issues about the use of non-custodial interrogations" in cases such as this (Gudjonsson 2003b: 581).

In January 2001, however, the prosecution's case would incur a setback, as further DNA analysis eliminated Rose as a suspect. Though the lack of physical evidence linking Rose to the murders significantly undermined the Crown's case, they still had Madonna Mary Kelly's testimony, the lynchpin that had led to the two earlier convictions. Yet after careful deliberation with the office of the B.C. Attorney General, the prosecution announced that it would no longer be proceeding with the case against Rose. In the opinion of Crown counsel, Gil McKinnon, Q.C., "to have a conviction against a person, I want to be very certain that that is the person who committed the offence" (Burke 2009). He went on to say that he would have been uncomfortable if a guilty verdict had been reached. After being confined almost ten years in prison for two murders he did not commit, Rose reestablished his relationship with his nineteen-year-old son and is on friendly terms with his son's mother, but he spends much of his time alone (Burke 2009).

Clayton George Mentuck

On July 13, 1996, members of various surrounding communities converged on the town of Rossburn, Manitoba, for the annual Harvest Festival Fair. Throughout the day residents took in activities, including the morning pancake breakfast, afternoon midway rides and visits to the petting zoo, quarterhorse and thoroughbred racing, and early evening chuckwagon races (*Mentuck* 2000b: para. 9). Following the last race of the evening, Amanda Cook's father searched the fairgrounds for her to no avail. He gathered that she had gotten a ride home with someone else, and he consequently left the fairgrounds without her (para. 11). The following day the fourteen-year-old was reported missing to the RCMP. On the morning of July 17, police discovered Amanda Cook's partially clad body, with a large rock placed on her head, in a boggy area near the fairgrounds (Makin 2000: A3; *Mentuck* 2000b: paras. 11, 26).

Clayton George Mentuck, a young Aboriginal man from the nearby Waywayseecappo Reserve who was at the Harvest Festival Fair on the day of the alleged offence, was suspected of being involved criminally in Cook's disappearance and death. As indicated by Makin (2000), the evidence against the accused "was startlingly thin" (A3). Mentuck was offered up as a suspect primarily because evidence indicated that he and the deceased were in each other's company throughout the day, although not in a one-on-one setting for any prolonged period of time (*Mentuck* 2000b: para. 13). No forensic evidence linked Mentuck to the victim or the crime scene (para. 18), and witnesses testified that the accused appeared normal and acted normally in the hours after the killing (para. 31). Counsel for the accused suggested that "The point of this investigation was ultimately not to gather evidence to determine who did it, but to create evidence to show that [Mentuck] did it" (Makin 2000: A3).

As noted by Mr. Justice MacInnes of the Manitoba Court of Queen's Bench, "this case has had a lengthy and arduous history" (2000b: para. 2). In April 1998, his colleague, Mr. Justice Menzies, ruled that Mentuck's statements to the police were inadmissible. The Crown was forced to stay the charges (*Mentuck* 2001: para. 3). Counsel for the accused had discovered that a significant portion of the videotape of Mr. Mentuck's police interrogation was missing. This fact was later confirmed by an RCMP lab in Ottawa. Moreover, Mr. Justice Menzies ruled that Mentuck's constitutionally enshrined right to silence was violated because police continued to question him even after asserting his right to silence seventy-five times (Makin 2000: A3). McIntyre (2006b: 137) suggests that "Mentuck talked about wanting to speak to a lawyer on nine separate occasions."

Following a stay of proceedings at the first trial, the RCMP, in an attempt to bolster their case against Mentuck, targeted him in a sophisticated undercover sting operation (*Mentuck* 2001: para. 4). The RCMP hired Douglas Brau, a man with a lengthy criminal record, to act as an informant and aide in the undercover operation (*Mentuck* 2000b: para. 74).[4] He was to visit Mentuck at the Brandon

Correctional Institute and sell him on the possibility of their working together in a sophisticated criminal organization following Mentuck's release from custody (para. 75). On the day of his release, Brau picked Mentuck up and the two travelled to a dwelling in Brandon, which was the RCMP's front house (para. 75).

Mentuck was introduced to RCMP officer UC1, who portrayed himself as Brau's boss in the criminal organization. As a sign of good faith, UC1 loaned Mentuck one hundred dollars to buy some new clothes, since his wardrobe consisted of what he was wearing upon his release from custody (para. 76). Undercover operatives were able to gain the target's confidence, and Mentuck was taken in by this crime boss ruse.

For the next seven days, Mentuck and his newfound friend completed tasks for the organization, including delivering parcels and counting large sums of money (*Mentuck* 2001: para. 4). Given the minimal time commitment (approximately twenty hours of work), the two were generously remunerated, Mentuck earning $1,800 (2000b: para. 76). The aim of this scheme was to impress upon Mentuck that as a member of the syndicate he could, over time, earn considerable sums of money. He would, though, have to come clean about his criminal past. Stressing that honesty, integrity, and loyalty were paramount to his membership in the criminal organization, the undercover officer encouraged Mentuck to tell him "exactly what he had done, both as proof to them of his honesty and so that they would be able to protect him and not be faced with any surprises result" (para. 77). Over the next few days the scenarios were configured so as to ensure lengthy one-on-one meetings between UC1 and Mentuck (para. 78). A front house was surreptitiously furnished with electronic surveillance equipment (audio and video) to monitor all activities and correspondence in the house, as well as "for the recording of telephone calls made from the residence" (para. 75). In a one-on-one meeting at the front house, Mentuck was told that the criminal organization had sources and that those sources indicated that Mentuck had committed the crime. The undercover operative continued to impress upon Mentuck that the organization did not care what he had done. Despite the officer's insistence that the organization knew that Mentuck was responsible for the death of Amanda Cook, Mentuck vehemently denied any participation in the murder, "upwards of a dozen times" (para. 57). The operatives then convinced Mentuck otherwise:

UC1: So you killed her?
Mentuck: I guess I must of 'cause I can't remember that part.
UC1: Well, we got to try to remember here George.
[There was then a period of silence]
UC1: We got to try to remember. How did you kill her?
Mentuck: They said I used a rock.
UC1: Well they said that. But how did you do it?
Mentuck: I don't know. (*Mentuck* 2000b: para. 81)

Despite suggestions from UC1 that the organization could cover things up and make this situation disappear, Mentuck avowed that all he knew about her death was "the result of things he'd been told or had seen in connection with the court proceedings" (Mentuck 2000b: para. 94).

In a further effort to obtain a confession, UC2, an RCMP corporal who purported to be UC1's superior, entered the front house and confronted UC1 about his ability to do his job, warning that if he was unable to get the necessary information from Mentuck about his involvement in the murder, his job with the organization would be in jeopardy (para. 81). He added that UC3, the criminal syndicate's kingpin, would be arriving in town the following day to meet the newest prospect. UC2 subsequently left the front house, where UC1 continued to grill Mentuck for details, this time adding that UC1's lucrative career with the organization was on the line and that he did not want to lose it. He added, "And I don't think you do either. Cause where the fuck are you gonna end up? Back on the reserve and back in jail. Do you want to do that? Huh? George do you want to do that?" (para. 81). Mentuck, in response, offered to return the previously earned money and purchased clothing and withdraw from the organization. However, UC1 "made clear to the accused that it wasn't that simple, that they were in this together and that if the accused were to step out, [UC1] would be out too" (para. 82). The following exchange then took place:

> UC1: You know… they know you killed her. You told me you killed her, but you're saying you don't remember. You gotta remember something George.
> Mentuck: I said, I guess I killed her.
> UC1: You guess?
> Mentuck: Yeah. 'Cause I don't fuckin' remember anything from the fuckin' night there. I just remember fuckin' leaving the grounds, being tripped, getting picked up on the road, going home, playing Nintendo and passed out.

UC1's efforts to elicit a confession from Mentuck, although persistent, proved futile. In a final attempt, Mentuck was taken by the primary undercover operative to a hotel in Winnipeg to meet UC3, the organization's big boss. To demonstrate the wealth and power of the organization, UC3 told Mentuck that it had arranged to have one of its confederates dying of cancer and AIDS take full responsibility for Cook's murder. As a result, this matter would come to an end: the police investigation against Mentuck would cease, and he would be cleared of any wrongdoing (para. 80). Moreover, the organization would help secure Mentuck's future by providing him with legal counsel and the necessary financing to institute legal proceedings against the Crown for having been wrongfully charged and imprisoned. UC3 emphasized, however, that the target would have to give explicit details about Cook's murder because the fall guy would likely undergo a series of extensive police interviews before his admission of guilt would be accepted (*Mentuck* 2000b: para.

90). This time Mentuck told the undercover operatives that he had killed Amanda with a rock because she would not stop pressuring him to have sex with her.

Once sufficient evidence against the accused was obtained by virtue of an undercover operation, the indictment against the accused was reinstated, with a second trial commencing in January 2000 (*Mentuck* 2001: para. 5). Having been unable to reach a verdict, the jury was discharged and a third trial proceeded in September 2000 before a judge alone (para. 7).

In his judgment, Mr. Justice MacInnes of the Manitoba Court of Queen's Bench found Clayton George Mentuck not guilty of the murder of Amanda Cook as charged. Having considered the totality of the evidence, including the circumstantial evidence (i.e., physical and scientific evidence), the evidence concerning opportunity, and the entire undercover sting operation, he concluded:

> the police must be aware that as the level of inducement increases, the risk of receiving a confession to an offence which one did not commit increases, and the reliability of the confession diminishes correspondingly. In this case, in my view, the level of inducement was overpowering... it provided nothing but upside for the accused to confess and a downside of frustration and despair in maintaining his denial. I conclude that the confession, if not false, is certainly too unreliable for acceptance as an admission of guilt. (*Mentuck* 2000b: para. 100)

Mr. Justice MacInnes described the killing of Amanda Cook as a "tragic event," but added that "at least equally tragic to the death of Amanda Cook... would be the wrongful conviction of one charged with her murder" (paras. 4–5).

Sometime after the Mr. Big sting, Mentuck was interviewed on the Bird Tail Sioux Reserve in Manitoba. Facing poverty and unemployment, he stated, he was an easy target for the undercover officers who "impressed him with expensive cars and wads of cash, and promised huge windfalls should he satisfy Mr. Big" (Hutchinson 2007).

Michael Bridges

Following the mysterious disappearance of Erin Chorney on April 21, 2002, police in Brandon, Manitoba, initiated a nationwide search. Crown prosecutor Bob Morrison said the disappearance "remained a compelling mystery for a long time" (MacAfee 2005a: A10). Though they initially treated it as a missing person case, police would soon have reason to suspect foul play. Weeks earlier, her ex-boyfriend, Michael Bradley Bridges, had been charged with assaulting Chorney, and he admitted to being the last person to see the victim (McIntyre 2006a: A9). As a result of the investigation that followed, Brandon Municipal Police suspected Bridges of being involved criminally in Chorney's disappearance, but lacked sufficient evidence to make a strong case against him. Investigators turned to the RCMP for help. In order to obtain vital evidence relating to Chorney's disappearance, the RCMP launched a four-month undercover operation involving fifteen undercover officers posing as members of a powerful and wealthy national criminal syndicate (MacAfee 2005b: A12). Having been somewhat burnt by the Mentuck case, the RCMP conducted this investigation with the assistance of Bob Morrison, "Manitoba's most senior Crown attorney" (McIntyre 2006b: 153–54), to ensure they "hadn't crossed any legal boundaries or done anything to jeopardize the status of any evidence they might dig up" (2006b: 212).

To initiate contact with the target, an undercover RCMP officer (an "attractive woman," according to McIntyre) (2006b: 125) posed as a marketing company representative, knocked on Bridges' door, and asked him to participate in a survey, which he did, despite initial reluctance. Shortly thereafter, he was notified that as a result of his participation in the survey he and the other "grand-prize winners," all undercover police officers, had won an all-expenses-paid trip to see an N.H.L. hockey game in Calgary. At the game, Bridges was introduced to one of the other winners, who claimed to belong to a successful criminal organization. The undercover officer befriended Bridges and successfully recruited him (*Bridges* 2005a: para. 3). Over time, Bridges would participate in a number of purported criminal activities for which he was paid lucratively.

From the onset, themes of honesty, loyalty, and truthfulness were repeatedly developed with the target. Bridges was led to believe that he was being recruited to join the organization, but that in order to be taken in as a member, he would be required to disclose details of his criminal past. Bridges was told that if he was honest and truthful, the boss of the organization, Mr. Big, could make his criminal problems disappear (para. 6). Only upon verification of the details, which would be cross-referenced with Mr. Big's extensive connections, would Bridges be made a member of the organization.

In a meeting that he thought was a dress rehearsal for a pending interview with the all-important crime boss, Bridges brought up the death of his ex-girlfriend. The undercover operative, posing as the main contact for the criminal organization, indicated to Bridges that the organization could retrieve the body from the burial site, dispose of the evidence, and create an alibi for Bridges at the time of the murder (*Bridges* 2005a: para. 19; MacAfee 2005b: A12).

Bridges carefully outlined his involvement in the murder of Erin Chorney, describing in detail how he planned to bury her in a recently excavated grave in a Brandon graveyard. He indicated that he had wrapped the body in a white, flat, unfitted bed sheet and buried Chorney face-up in the centre of the grave. He also told the undercover investigators the type of shovel he had used (MacAfee 2005b: A12). McIntyre (2006b) later wrote that the body was "face down with an electrical cord wrapped around her torso… a fitted white sheet was around the body. The remnants of Saran Wrap were around her head and hair" (357–58). According to Mr. Justice Menzies, "much evidence was heard as to the emphasis placed on the necessity of telling the truth if one wanted to be a member of this organization" (*Bridges* 2005a: para. 15). Consequently, "the motive which caused him to confess would also operate as the motive which caused him to tell the truth" (para. 19). A noteworthy fact is that the police located the body of the deceased *only after* receiving the information from Bridges. Had it not been for the elaborate undercover investigation employed by the RCMP, the murder of Erin Chorney might still be unsolved. In the end, a jury convicted Michael Bradley Bridges of first-degree murder (*Bridges* 2006).

In some respects, Bridges might be considered the "poster boy" case for support for the RCMP's Mr. Big operation. Defence counsel did, however, appeal the jury's first-degree murder verdict, arguing that Bridges had exaggerated his confession about the killing making it appear to be planned and that the trial judge had misdirected the jury on first-degree murder. Bridges' appeal was dismissed (2006). The question still remains, was this really a first-degree murder case?

The above three cases illustrate both the dangers and the allure of Mr. Big undercover investigations. The risk of false confessions and wrongful convictions, however, is high and will be discussed further in Chapter 2. The three cases also expose the general format of a Mr. Big operation, which will be discussed in further detail in Chapter 3. Chapter 4 examines some of the legal and moral issues arising out of Mr. Big undercover operations, and Chapter 5 explores some of the possible solutions to their dangers. The remainder of this chapter sketches out the origins of Mr. Big and its script, court challenges to the secrecy surrounding Mr. Big, the prevalence and price of the operation, its use outside of Canada, and the methodology used in this present study of eighty-one cases of Mr. Big in Canada.

The Origins of Mr. Big and Its Script

The first reported Mr. Big operation in Canada, although it was not called by that name, was probably the case against Mr. Todd in 1901 in Manitoba. Faced with an unsolved murder, the chief of police employed two men as detectives to see if they could procure evidence against Todd. The two detectives pretended to Todd "that they belonged to a gang of organized criminals, from the operations of which large profits were likely to be made, and they offered to make him a member of the gang if he would satisfy them that he had committed some serious crime; and it was by the influence of this inducement that the prisoner confessed" to one of the detectives (para. 15). Mr. Justice Dubuc described the evidence gathering operation as "vile," "base," and "contemptible" (paras. 3 and 8). Apparently, the tactics were so embarrassing to the Crown that he did not support the admissibility of the statement and stated that there should be a new trial in which the Crown would not tender evidence of the confession. However, the Crown was not prepared to concede that the statement was inadmissible in law, and so the Court went on to decide its admissibility (*Todd* 1901: para. 13). The court found that the detective was not a person in authority and since there were no charges at the time the detective could hardly be said to have induced a confession in relation to outstanding charges. The Court went on to say that the trial judge was correct in admitting the evidence and confirmed the conviction (paras. 11 and 23).

The case of *Beaulac* in 1988 was, perhaps, a precursor to the Mr. Big investigative technique.[5] An undercover officer who was working in the drug squad at the time of the investigation posed as a gangster and got Beaulac to confess to the brutal murder of a young woman in 1981 (para. 9 and 11). Beaulac testified at his trial that his confession was mere boasting in order to be accepted into the undercover officer's fabricated gang (para. 13). It is unclear as to whether the Beaulac investigation fits within the well-orchestrated scenarios that the police developed in the early 1990s; however, one source identifies it as the first Mr. Big operation, claiming this "tradecraft... has solved hundreds of murders across Canada, and a growing number around the world" (Lions Gate Investigations Group 2009).[6]

In 2004, when he was asked about this interrogation technique, Al Haslett, an RCMP sergeant based in Kelowna, British Columbia who has been credited as one of its pioneering architects, responded: "I was probably the one who started it... I was just thinking outside the box, trying to see how far we could go" (Hutchinson 2004: RB1). This study addresses the question, just how far will they go? It is unlikely that Haslett was aware that he was, as Mr. Justice Rosenberg suggests, reviving an ancient technique (*Osmar* 2007a: para. 1), which over one hundred years earlier the Manitoba Court of King's Bench had described as vile and contemptible.

Some academics suggest that police investigations in many countries have moved from coercion to deception in order to investigate serious criminal behaviour effectively in the face of a progressively more regulated custodial investigative environment (Bronitt 2004: 36; Leo 1992; Ross 2008b: 451–52).[7] In Canada, the RCMP has creatively fashioned a controversial undercover interrogation technique that maintains aspects of coercion and adds further deception to their pre-custody investigations. The "Mr. Big" scenario, also referred to as the "crime boss" scenario, "the advanced homicide undercover technique" (Gorbet 2004: 54), and the "major crime homicide technique" (RCMP 2009), enables the police to circumvent many of the procedural and evidentiary rules that govern their investigations once a suspect is taken into custody (Bronitt 2004: 36; *Evans* 1996: para. 36; Leo 1992: 43). Investigators claim to turn to this investigative technique in a last resort effort to obtain incriminating evidence in the form of a confession from a suspect in investigations of serious crimes that have reached an impasse (*Osmar* 2007a: para. 1). When police have eliminated all other suspects but are unable to obtain sufficient evidence to support a charge against a suspect, this investigative procedure can produce sufficient evidence to substantiate a charge against a suspect, identify additional suspects in the criminal investigations, or eliminate a suspect from suspicion (*Dix* 2001: para. 14; *Skinner* 1993: para. 7).

The Mr. Big tactic is usually a three-stage process of "introduction, credibility-building and evidence-gathering" (Fournier 2009: A9), where operatives continuously interchange roles as passive observers and active participants. After following a target for some time in order to gather information about that person's daily habits (Baron 2008b: A8; Cherry 2005: A8; *Evans* 1996: para. 5; *Hart* 2007: para. 18; *Lepage* 2003: para. 14; *Macki* 2001: para. 9), the police develop an interactive scenario. An undercover officer who has participated in over one hundred Mr. Big stings said, "We definitely get as much detail as we can about the target, so we know, for the most part, how we should be acting around him or her. Everything is thought out methodically" (Baron 2008b: A8). Marx (1988) indicates that a suspect's behaviour will be conditioned by what the environment offers (72). In some instances, the police will consult with behavioural profilers, psychologists, and forensic psychiatrists about the personality and behaviour of the target. These experts can help undercover operatives assume the personae of criminals who can interact with the accused (*Griffin* 2001: para. 39; *Osmar* 2001: para. 35). This stage of the operation can take weeks or even months to complete (Baron 2008b: A8). What's more, some targets can be under surveillance and subjected to having their conversations intercepted during this stage of the undercover operation (*Roberts* 1997: para. 3).

The thrust of a Mr. Big scenario is to have a number of undercover police officers adopt fictitious criminal personae, pose as organized crime figures, and deceive the suspect into believing he or she is being conditioned to join an intricate and highly successful criminal syndicate under the direction of Mr. Big, the boss of the enterprise (*Bicknell* 2003: para. 94; *Dix* 2002: para. 119). An offer of a lucrative career in organized crime is held out to the suspect on the condition that the crime boss is "satisfied of [his or her] honesty and trustworthiness" (*Skiffington* 2004: para. 10). Indeed, the RCMP has perfected a backdrop that simulates a real-world criminal environment in which undercover agents are enmeshed both directly and surreptitiously with the criminal underworld, so much so that fantasy is difficult to differentiate from reality. The verisimilitude of their performance is gripping. Hank Reiner, a British Columbia prosecutor, commented on the undercover sting operation, saying, "If you are going to pretend that you are a member of a gang, you have to adopt the colouration of the gang" (Baron 2008d: A10). Closing the gaps between appearance and reality, a well-executed simulated event becomes the reflection of its reality, preventing the viewer from distinguishing the real from the simulated (see Bogard 1996).

RCMP operatives endeavour to establish their credibility as members of a criminal organization (*MacMillan* 2000: para. 23). Intrinsic to the success of the operation (i.e., obtaining a confession from the target) is the "carefully structured relationship" that develops between the target and the undercover operators (*Evans* 1996: para. 28). Such bonding or grooming can include spending time together "drinking and watching strippers, discussing sexual exploits in the grossest possible language" (*Evans* 1996: para. 7), and telling their targets about their own criminal behaviour.

In recent Mr. Big stings, undercover officers have been more careful at the evidence-gathering stage to articulate that the organization demands honesty, trust, dependability, and loyalty as hallmark requirements for membership (*MacMillan* 2000: para. 58). Equally important, undercover operatives in some cases clearly articulate to targets that they are free to come and go, and can withdraw from the organization at any time (*McIntyre* 1993: para. 55).

The scenarios consist of a series of lucrative, yet staged, criminal activities and tasks that the target performs for the gang (*Bicknell* 2003: para. 93). These criminal tasks give credence to the legitimacy of the criminal enterprise. As the scenarios progress, the target is engaged in "a simulated and progressively escalating series of criminal activities" (*Cretney* 1999: para. 12) and, correspondingly, is offered increasing responsibility and monetary rewards (*Bicknell* 2003: para. 96; Nowlin 2004: 384). The staged criminal activities of the criminal syndicate are wide-ranging, including but not limited to picking up and dropping off parcels, acting as a lookout during various criminal transactions, delivering vehicles, counting large sums of money, drug trafficking, selling and distributing firearms, feigning contract killings (murder for hire), forcibly collecting unpaid debts, breaking and entering, and selling and distributing contraband (*Caster* 1998: para. 19; Gorbet 2004: 55; *Grandinetti* 2005: para. 8; *Hart* 2007: para. 17; *Joseph* 2000a: para. 40; *Proulx* 2005: para. 11).[8] If necessary, undercover police officers will resort to more aggressive scenarios, including feigned murders, staged kidnappings, and beatings, to project a convincing image of corruption (Baron 2008a: A4; Hutchinson 2004: RB1; McIntyre 2006b). Examples of these types of scenarios are found in *Dix* (2002), *Terrico* (2005a), *Roberts* (1997) and *Bridges* (as discussed in McIntyre 2006b: 205–10).

The undercover operation is aimed at making targets believe they can be up-and-comers in the criminal organization, but only if they first confirm their loyalty by disclosing details of a criminal past (*Bicknell* 2003: para. 94; *Unger* 1993a: para. 21; Stueck 2008: A3.). Typically, the undercover investigation culminates in a meeting, akin to a job interview, in which the target is introduced to and interviewed by Mr. Big, the commanding boss of the fictional criminal syndicate (*Bicknell* 2003: para. 103; *Peterffy* 2000: para. 6). He "is a shape-shifter, a chameleon. He moves with ease between our everyday world and the world of violence and darkness beneath" (Baron 2008b: A8). Although a fiction, Mr. Big is a professional inter-rogator charged with the task of eliciting inculpatory statements from the target about his or her criminal past. He is portrayed as an all-powerful individual who has extensive connections, ranging from the criminal underworld to reliable police sources and various other criminal justice officials. He "projects confidence. His naturally serious manner edges toward menacing. This is a man who brooks no nonsense" (Baron 2008b: A8).

With an uncompromisingly forthright attitude, the crime boss expresses concern about the target's criminal past, especially about anything that could jeopardize the integrity or the existence of the organization, such as the target's involvement in the alleged crime and serious criminal investigations that might generate police attention (Staples 2009a: A1). Generally, the target is shown a purportedly official police document indicating that he or she is the focus of a serious criminal investigation and that an arrest is imminent. Mr. Big outlines a scheme that he assures will help the target avoid criminal prosecution, provided the target is entirely forthcoming about his or her involvement in the ongoing investigation. Targets with outstanding charges (known as "heat") are of no value to the organization. Once more, the boss reiterates the importance of trust, honesty, and loyalty, attributes the organization demands from its members (*MacMillan* 2000a: para. 52). Moreover, the boss advises the target that he will use his "sources," which permeate all levels of the criminal justice system, to check the veracity of all statements given to him (*Simmonds* 2002: para. 32). For example, in *Giroux* (2007) the undercover officer stated, "Tell me what happened 'cause I know what happened. I'm testing you right now to see if you're a liar or if you're ... solid. [pause] There's nowhere's ... nowhere's where I haven't been before okay?" (para. 92). Upon verification of the target's story, Mr. Big promises not only help making the "problem" go away, but also membership in the criminal organization and great financial gain (*Skiffington* 2004: para. 34). These later interviews are usually audio-video recorded and tendered as evidence at trial.

Lifting the Shroud of Secrecy Surrounding Mr. Big

Historically, details concerning intelligence matters in Canada have been left unspoken at almost all levels of civic discourse (Security Intelligence Review Committee 2005). They are customarily shrouded in secrecy (Marx 1988: 15). Indeed, the enigmatic and classified nature of undercover work is the cornerstone of its very success (Ross 2008a: 469). However, critics have argued that restricting the public's access to information about how the RCMP conducts criminal investigations prevents public scrutiny and oversight, and it perpetuates an uncritical attitude. Mulgrew (2007: B1) suggests that arguments in favour of a veil of secrecy surrounding RCMP operational methods are rhetoric "designed to prevent public discussion and oversight" about the activities of government officials. Reflecting a similar sentiment, Rob Anderson, a lawyer for the *Vancouver Sun*, says that to enshroud in secrecy information related to these operational methods would "criminalize public discussion about the policies and practices of the police and the functioning of the criminal courts" (Tibbetts 2001: A3). Political studies Professor Emeritus C.E.S. Franks, of Queen's University, warns about the dangers that stem from a culture of secrecy: "Secrecy in any government agency is an invitation to an abuse of power, and there is therefore a potential threat to free discussions and democratic politics" (Security Intelligence Review Committee 2005: 8).

Applications for sweeping publication bans by the RCMP were once routinely made to protect information related to the identity of undercover operatives involved in these covert operations, as well as details of the undercover techniques employed by the police (*O.N.E.* 2000b: para. 3). As Hutchinson (2007) indicates, these bans placed "very narrow limits on what the media could report" (A1). In *Mentuck* (2000a), for example, lawyers on behalf of the RCMP applied for a ban on the publication of information related to the identity of the RCMP operatives and the specific operational methods employed by officers in the investigation of Mentuck. Law enforcement officials expressed concern that "the techniques used in this case have taken years to develop and refine for use in undercover operations," and that lifting the cloak of secrecy on the Mr. Big technique might very well expose potential targets to sensitive information, thus rendering the technique "ineffective or less effective in the pursuit of criminals" (*Mentuck* 2000a: para. 8).

Upon reviewing the stated law (i.e., *Dagenais v. Canadian Broadcasting Corp.* 1994), Mr. Justice Menzies (in *Mentuck*) dismissed an application to ban the publication of the specific undercover techniques because a ban would effectively curtail "the rights of the press to report on the trial proceedings and the right of the accused to a fair trial" (2000a: para. 9). He did, however, prohibit for a period of one year the publication of the names and identities of the undercover police officers involved in the investigation and any information that could publicly identify the RCMP operatives (para. 13). He went on to say that preventing the dissemination of information related to police investigative techniques would fundamentally shelter the RCMP from "the penetrating light of public scrutiny" (para. 10).

On further appeal to the Supreme Court of Canada, Mr. Justice Iacobucci, for the Court, highlighted the importance of balancing "the interests of the public in ensuring effective policing and society's fundamental interest in allowing the public to monitor the police, as well as the right of the accused to a 'fair and public hearing'" (*Mentuck* 2001: para. 1). In a unanimous decision, the Court affirmed the order of the Manitoba Court of Queen's Bench to lift the publication ban on the RCMP operational methods because "the deleterious effects [of a ban] on the rights protected by ss. 2(b) and 11(d) of the Canadian Charter of Rights and Freedoms" would outweigh any efficacy the ban might have on police investigations (*Mentuck* 2001: para. 2). The Court ruled that insulating police conduct from public scrutiny "seriously deprives the Canadian public of its ability to know of and be able to respond to police practices that, left unchecked, could erode the fabric of Canadian society and democracy" (para. 51).[9]

In a more recent decision, Mme. Justice Humphries imposed the following publication ban, referring to the wording as "standard for orders of this type" (*Black* 2007: para. 2):

This court orders a ban on and prohibits the publication in print and the broadcasting on television, film, radio and the Internet of any information tending or serving to publicly identify the undercover police officers in the investigation of the accused in this matter, including but not limited to, any

likeness of the officers, the appearance of their attire and their physical description, for a period of five years. (para. 1)

She imposed a $2000 fine on CHBC Television for violating the publication ban.

In an antithetical, or perhaps cooperative move, the RCMP now grants public access to this exclusive criminal underworld. RCMP Superintendent Lorne Schwartz,
head of B.C. undercover operations, explains the reason for this:

> Any time you run a covert operation, the public wants to know what's going
> on. That's public money going into this, and not a lot of information coming
> out. The truth of the matter is we don't want to talk about it, but we felt the
> need to be somewhat accountable, a little more transparent. We want to as-
> sure the public that when we do these [Mr. Big stings], we're trying to solve
> crime. (Dawson 2008: A4)

The Prevalence and Price of Mr. Big

The RCMP website states that as of 2008 it had employed this undercover operation on 350 occasions, that the suspect was cleared or charged in 75 percent of the
investigations, and that 25 percent remained unresolved (RCMP 2009). Following
an Access to Information Request, the RCMP employee was unable to clarify what
percentage was charged and what percentage was cleared (Yan 2009). According
to a lawyer representing the RCMP, the target is charged in 75 percent of the Mr.
Big operations that are conducted and cleared of responsibility in only a handful
of cases (Baron 2008a: A4). Again, it is unclear what number amounts to a "handful of cases."

The conviction rate of those cases that go to trial is a remarkable 95 percent
(Baron 2008a: A4; RCMP 2009). At present, there is no annual report or organized
public database that tracks the frequency or outcome of Mr. Big undercover operations. Following an Access to Information Request, we were told no statistics
are kept on this investigative technique and the RCMP would have to request files
from all of its divisions. Once the boxes of material arrived for review and we paid
a research fee (ten dollars per hour), we might still receive no information, as most
of the information in the files would likely be considered personal (Beauchamp
2009).

The media and others have reported the cost of Mr. Big in a small number
of such operations, but there is no consistency in what is included in the costs.
Powell and Rusnell (1999: F1) reported that a 1994 undercover investigation
undertaken by the Sherwood Park police detachment targeting Jason Dix came
with price tag of $137,000. Lasting thirteen months, the operating costs covered
miscellaneous expenses, and did not include salaries or overtime of the 52 police
officers involved in the undercover operation. Brautigam (2007a: 16) reported
that the elaborate four-month sting operation launched to recruit Nelson Hart

into a fictitious criminal syndicate ended up costing $413,000. Following the March 2005 murder of four RCMP officers in Mayerthorpe, Alberta, the RCMP initiated a three-year, $2 million undercover operation to find the person(s) who allegedly aided James Roszko, the man responsible for the shootings (Libin 2009: A15). Kari (2006: S1) reported that the RCMP spent $4 million in trying to elicit a confession from Salvatore Ciancio for the drug-related murders of two Burnaby residents in 1995 and five people in Abbotsford in 1996; however, at Ciancio's trial on the two Burnaby murders, the judge found the evidence "cryptic, confusing and not subject to a single interpretation" (*Ciancio* 2006: para. 263), and he acquitted Ciancio. The trial judge in *Cretney* (1999: para. 7) stated that the budget for the operation included $1500 for liquor. Maidment (2009: 101) reports that sixteen RCMP officers were employed over two years in a $1.6 million operation against Wade Skiffington. Although we made a request through Access to Information, the RCMP was unable to provide us with the costs associated with Mr. Big operations.

Mr. Big Outside of Canada

In the early 1990s, just as Mr. Big undercover operations were getting into full swing in Canada, Colin Stagg was subject to a "honey-trap" operation in England, in which a female undercover police officer conned him into talking about violent sexual fantasies. The operation led to Stagg's being charged for the murder of twenty-three-year-old Rachel Nickell in front of her two-year-old son. At Stagg's trial, the judge excluded the honey-trap evidence, condemning the undercover operation as "deceptive conduct of the grossest kind." Stagg, who had spent thirteen months in custody, was paid £706,000 in compensation. The man who later pleaded guilty to manslaughter in the death of Rachel Nickell, Robert Napper, had murdered another woman in front of her child after the killing of Nickell (Cheston and Davenport 2008; BBC News 2008). Physical evidence, including DNA evidence, clearly linked Napper to Nickell's murder (Edwards and Rayner 2008). Despite this miscarriage of justice, some news media portray this case as a shadow hanging over the English justice system that will prevent the admission of evidence from other honey trap operations (Palmer 2008).[10]

In the United States, once suspects are read their *Miranda* rights deception, with few restrictions, is an acceptable investigative tool to elicit a confession. Obviously, police impersonation of lawyers or ministers is unacceptable; but lying about the existing evidence is acceptable (Ross 2008a: 452–53). Confessions must be voluntary; however, the voluntariness standard in the United States has been described as "notoriously forgiving and vague" (Garrett 2009: in press). Undercover Mr. Big scenarios are not permitted because they are considered coercive and an infringement of a suspect's constitutional rights (Hutchinson 2007: A1; Kari 2006: S1; Seyd 2007: 23). The deception that takes place during in-custody interrogations is usually acceptable because the accused has been read his or her rights.

Despite the restrictions in England, where the "rules and practices with respect to undercover operations limit the police more than do those rules and practices in Canada" (*Proulx* 2005: para. 37), Canadian police officers were permitted to conduct a Mr. Big investigation on a target in Great Britain (Proulx), with the assistance of local authorities, in order to gather evidence for a trial that was held in Canada. In another case involving Canadian citizens Sebastian Burns and Atif Rafay, Mr. Big evidence gathered in Canada was used to convict suspects tried in the United States.

In March 1995, RCMP discovered the body of Stacey Koehler in the base-ment of her parents' home in Burnaby, British Columbia (Hunter 2003: A20). A co-worker, Michael Proulx, was suspected of being involved in her death, but he provided authorities with an alibi. The alibi was later discovered to be false, but by that time Proulx had fled to Mexico and subsequently settled in England. Still believing him to be the murderer, investigators felt their only option was to mount an undercover investigation with Proulx as the target. Under the strict guidance and direction of British authorities, Canadian officers conducted a Mr. Big operation and were able to successfully obtain a confession. British authorities subsequently arrested Proulx "on a provisional warrant issued pursuant to the United Kingdom Extradition Act" (*Proulx* 2005: para. 20). He was then read his rights by RCMP officers and placed on a plane bound for Canada (para. 54).

In Canada, Proulx sought to exclude the self-incriminating statements made to undercover officers in England based on the notion that evidence obtained in a foreign jurisdiction should be ruled inadmissible as evidence at trial. Without deciding whether it would have been admissible in England, B.C. Supreme Court Justice Paul Williamson ruled that the Mr. Big undercover operation would not shock "a reasonable, dispassionate person in [Canada], aware of the circumstances surrounding this case," and it was "hardly so grossly unfair as to repudiate the values underlying our trial system" (para. 52). He ruled the evidence admissible at trial (para. 52). Proulx pleaded guilty to second-degree murder and was sentenced to life with no parole eligibility for thirteen years (Fraser 2005: A8).

Ironically, evidence from a Mr. Big operation in Canada was used against an accused charged with murder in the United States (where evidence from Mr. Big operations is generally not admissible). In the early hours of July 13, 1994, Bellevue police in Washington State were called to the Rafay residence, where inside the house police discovered the bodies of Tariq and Sultana Rafay, as well as their daughter Basma, who was barely clinging to life (*United States of America v. Burns* 1997: para. 3).[11] Investigators immediately suspected Atif Rafay, son of Tariq and Sultana, and Atif's close friend Sebastian Burns of the murders, but they lacked sufficient evidence to support a charge against the two men. At the time of the murders, both co-accused "lived in West Vancouver and were at the material times Canadian citizens" (para. 2). Investigators alleged that the conspiracy to commit the murders occurred there as well (Baron 2008c: A11).

When Burns and Rafay returned home to Vancouver from Bellevue, the

RCMP proposed joining forces with the Bellevue detectives under the *Mutual Legal Assistance in Criminal Matters Act* (Cooper 2007). The RCMP mounted an elaborate Mr. Big undercover operation and obtained self-incriminating statements from both suspects. With assurances from Washington state prosecutors that the two men would not face execution if convicted, Canadian authorities extradited the alleged murderers to Washington State to face three counts of first-degree murder. The confessions elicited from this covert investigation were admissible as evidence at their trial. The accused were convicted and are now trying to establish that they were wrongfully convicted.[12]

The High Court of Australia heard four cases in which Mr. Big scenarios,[13] imported from Canada (*Tofilau* 2007: para. 5) were used to elicit confessions from four men individually accused of killing various people. Although the decision was split, the majority of the court found that the undercover police officers were not persons in authority. Citing the Supreme Court of Canada in *Grandinetti* (2005), the Chief Justice found that the undercover police officers were not persons in authority even though they claimed to be able to influence the authorities (paras. 12–13), and that the deception and tricks used were not such that they would have overborne the will of the accused. Therefore, their confessions were voluntary and properly admitted by the trial judges (para. 22).

A Study of 81 Canadian Cases of Mr. Big Operations

How should one approach the study of Mr. Big investigations? In commenting on research conducted on wrongful convictions, Leo and Gould (2009) point out that legal research on the topic differs from social science research. More specifically, "to the extent that legal scholarship has a methodology, it is case-based description, analysis, and prescription" (2009: 14). Such narratives (as illustrated in our introduction to this chapter) "are powerful and compelling vehicles for communicating injustices" (14) or other stories about legal phenomena. While social scientists study cases, they are more likely to treat cases as "sources of data" rather than as the basis for a methodology, and they are also more likely to examine a larger number of cases to systematically decipher possible patterns and explanations (17). As Mary Jane Mossman points out, lawyers are more likely to *search* out cases as a problem-solving activity, looking for the appropriate principles to be applied to certain fact patterns or evaluating decisions to see if they conform to principles of law. Social scientists are more likely to *research* a problem from a critical and inclusive perspective (1993: 157–58). For example, lawyers are trained to look for what is "relevant"; they often do not count what they consider to be irrelevant. Social scientists, on the other hand, view the legally irrelevant as relevant to their research (see Brockman and Chunn 1993: 12–13).

Although we embed our research in much of the wrongful conviction literature (next Chapter), we do not, as many researchers on wrongful convictions do, restrict our cases to the wrongfully convicted (Leo and Gould 2009: 20–21). However, this book takes up only a small part of the challenge that Leo (2005) and Leo and Gould (2009) make to researchers on wrongful convictions. There is much research left to be conducted on the Mr. Big technique.

We have drawn on our backgrounds in both the social sciences and law to carry out this research. First, we conducted what Leo and Gould (2009: 19–20) describe as the aggregated case study approach, in which social science researchers systematically bring cases together, code common variables, and run a descriptive analysis of what a particular social phenomenon looks like — in this case the Mr. Big investigative technique (see Chapter 3). We also examine Mr. Big from a legal perspective (in Chapters 4 and 5).

The purpose of this study is to turn investigative eyes on the highly controversial Mr. Big undercover investigative technique that has come to exist as a legitimate tool used by the RCMP and other police forces across Canada. This study analyzes eighty-one legal decisions in which a confession obtained from a Mr. Big investigation was tendered as evidence against the accused (See Appendix A for a list of the cases). There were a total of ninety-three individual accused persons in these eighty-one cases. These cases include all the available court decisions between the first known court case in 1992 and January 2010. The eighty-one reasons for judgment were systematically identified through Quicklaw and other databases such as Canadian provincial and territorial law court websites and Canadian Legal Information Institute (CanLII).

Initial search parameters used to select the legal decisions were the key words "Mr. Big," "Big Boss," and "Crime Boss." These search terms were also entered into the Québec judgments database. However, the one case emanating from Québec, *Lepage* (2005a and b), did not refer to Mr. Big *per se*. Additional searches with the recurring terms from that case — for example, "l'opération d'infiltration" and "un(e) agent(e) d'infiltration" — yielded no further cases.

While these terms formed a consistently applied criterion for inclusion, they were not present in every decision. Nonetheless, each decision typically included sufficient details about the undercover ruse, which allowed it to be identified as a Mr. Big case. For example, in *Simmonds* (2000a), Mr. Justice Smith described the Mr. Big strategy without using the search words:

> In January 1999, the R.C.M.P. implemented an undercover police operation with Mr. Simmonds as the target. The undercover operators portrayed themselves to Mr. Simmonds as being part of a sophisticated criminal organization. During a series of meetings between January and April 1999, Mr. Simmonds was included in discussions, plans and assignments for a variety of fictitious criminal transactions, some of which had the appearance of involving guns and drugs. (para. 7)

While legal databases are a "fruitful source of data for analysis" (Palys 2003: 240), case law analysis has limitations. Not every case that appears before the judiciary is entered into the database. According to Busby (2000: para. 11), "judicial practices on the publication of reasons vary across Canada." Formal written reasons for trial decisions are issued in only a small number of cases; they are generally provided orally and are rarely transcribed (Busby 2000: para. 11). In addition, little is reported when the accused are tried by a jury. Moreover, cases where guilty pleas are entered are generally excluded from these databases unless a sentencing decision is published. Therefore, this book does not cover every single Mr. Big operation. Some of these operations resulted in a "clearing" of the target as a suspect without any public documentation, and some operations were halted because of threats to agents or targets becoming suspicious of the undercover police officers (see McIntyre 2006b: 143–44, and *Dix* 2001: paras. 15–19 for examples).

In order to supplement the cases, journalistic reports were accessed through two electronic databases: *Canadian Newsstand* and CBCA *Current Events*, both of which provide a broad scope of Canadian current events and full text of over 150 Canadian newspapers from Canada's leading publishers. Media reports provided insight into the fundamental mechanics and historical context of Mr. Big, and also contained additional information not provided in the legal judgements. In addition, the recent coverage in television media, namely investigative reports from Canadian and American television networks (i.e., CBC's *The Fifth Estate*, CTV's *W-5*, and CBS's *48 Hours Mystery*), proved to be valuable sources of information regarding the Mr. Big technique. These secondary sources were used to supplement, not supplant, the original criminal cases. Like Drizin and Leo's approach (2004: 927), media details were compared to what was contained in the legal judgements. For the most part, news media reports were factually consistent with the legal judgements. We did not order transcripts from all preliminary hearings and trials, because the cost would have been prohibitive; however, in some cases we made use of transcripts available through other sources.

It should be noted that these person-to-person murders, which were the subject of all but four of the Mr. Big operations in this study,[14] are only a small fraction of the murders that take place in Canada, even though they seem to consume the bulk of police resources and media attention. Corporate crimes resulting in death appear not to receive the same amount of attention, investigation, or research (Boyd, Chunn, and Menzies 2002; McMullan 2005; Snider 2000; Tataryn 1979; Tombs and Whyte 2003).

Focusing on police investigations of specific murder cases (those using Mr. Big investigative techniques) often leaves one with little understanding of the big picture — much like the tunnel vision that sometimes leads to police targeting specific suspects or a neglect of the social and economic circumstances of those who are targeted. In analyzing murder statistics in England between 1993 and 2000, Dorling found that despite overall falling murder rates, murder rates of men born in 1965 or later were increasing (2004: 189). Most of these men had left school in the summer of 1981 at the age of sixteen. Poor men were unable to find decent employment in 1981 and thereafter because of government policies. Dorling writes,

> Behind the man with a knife is the man who sold him the knife, the man who did not give him a job, the man who decided that his school did not need funding, the man who closed down the branch plant where he could have worked, the man who decided to reduce benefit levels so that a black economy grew, all the way back to the woman who only noticed 'those inner cities' some six years after the summer of 1981, and the people who voted to keep her in office. (2004: 191)

Many murder suspects in Canada may be cut from the same cloth, yet this contextual background is sometimes lost. To the extent possible, we try to provide the backgrounds of the Mr. Big targets discussed in this book. As conservative and "liberal" policies (e.g., those of the Liberal government in British Columbia) put more and more people on the unemployment lines in Canada, we too might experience an increase in the murder rate in a particular demographic cohort.

Notes

1. Mr. Justice MacInnes was appointed to the Manitoba Court of Appeal in 2007; <www.manitobacourts.mb.ca/ca/ca_judges.html> accessed June 19, 2009.
2. UC (undercover) replaces the names of undercover officers in this book because some names are under publication bans. If there is more than one undercover agent, UC1 and UC2 are used.
3. In *Burlingham*, the Supreme Court of Canada noted that s. 10(b) of the *Canadian Charter of Rights and Freedoms* "specifically prohibits the police … from belittling an accused's lawyer with the express goal or effect of undermining the accused's confidence in and relationship with defence counsel (1995: para. 14). However, since Andrew Rose was not being detained or under arrest at the material time, this restriction did not apply to the undercovers' interrogations.
4. In exchange for his part in the ruse, Brau received a payment of $25,000 and had the potential to net an additional $25,000 for relocation purposes (*Mentuck* 2000b: para. 74).
5. Although Maidment (2009: 23, 85, and 88) claims that this investigative tactic has been used by the RCMP since the 1970s, she does not provide any evidence or cases of this practice in the 1970s or 1980s. It is true that undercover police officers posed as drug dealers to elicit confessions from detainees (see for example, *Miller and Cockriell* 1975: para. 13 and 25); however, these too appear as precursors to the elaborate schemes behind present day Mr. Big operations.
6. One source claims that this blog was written by a former senior RCMP officer with considerable experience with this technique, and in the blog he claims to have participated in over forty Mr. Big confessions.
7. In his acclaimed book *Undercover: Police Surveillance in America,* Marx (1988) states, "There is an interesting irony at work here: restrict police use of coercion, and the use of deception increases" (47).
8. These undercover operatives often create the appearance of breaking the law; however,

according to Gorbet, the improprieties police encourage or actively participate in are usually lawful: "The general premise which runs throughout this technique is that no real crime is committed. All of the participants, except the target, are police officers and the actions committed are fake and only intended to emulate the crime. Through the use of control of the target and numerous undercover operators, the police can effectively emulate a range of criminal activity" (2004: 56). There are, however, occasions when the undercover officers encourage or condone breaking the law, such as drinking alcohol contrary to a target's probation order. We return to Gorbet's premise in Chapter 4.

9. The Victorian Court of Appeal in Australia reached a similar conclusion, stating that the manner in which evidence "comes into existence, and the procedures followed by investigative agencies are themselves matters of considerable public importance" (quoted in Palmer 2005: 111).

10. In earlier decisions, English courts had ruled that evidence of undercover police officers posing as buyers for stolen jewelry and stolen vehicles was inadmissible (R. v. Christou [1992] 4 All ER 559, [1992] 3 WLR 228; R. v. Bryce [1992] 4 All ER 567, 95 Cr App Rep 320). In Christou, the court wrote, "It would be wrong for police officers to adopt or use an undercover pose or disguise to enable themselves to ask questions about an offence uninhibited by the requirements of the code and with the effect of circumventing it" (1992: 566).

11. Basma Rafay would later succumb to her injuries.

12. Sebastian Burns and Atif Rafay have established an appeal campaign. See <www.rafayburnsappeal.com>. In addition, Burns' sister, Tiffany, produced a documentary chronicling both the Mr. Big scenario and the alleged wrongful conviction of both her brother and Atif Rafay. See <www.mrbigthemovie.com>.

13. In Australia, the Mr. Big technique is sometimes referred to as the "Canadian Model" (Palmer 2005: 111).

14. See the cases of Carter (2001), Joseph (2000), Porsch (2007), and Steadman (2008a).

2

False Confessions and Wrongful Convictions

The list of wrongfully convicted individuals is growing rapidly; so, too, is the literature on wrongful convictions in Canada and elsewhere (see, for example, Anderson and Anderson 2009; Bellemare and Finlayson 2004; Denov and Campbell 2005; Dufraimont 2008; Macfarlane 2006; and Maidment 2009). Siegel suggests that wrongful conviction scholarship and advocacy are moving into a third wave. The first wave involved the use of modern science such as DNA evidence to exonerate people who were convicted before such evidence was available. The second wave exposed faulty police practices, which produced, for example, eye witness errors and in-custody false confessions. It was believed that these errors could be corrected through the introduction of better procedures. Following the pattern of wrongful convictions, Siegel suggests that the third wave should be concerned with structural features that operate "outside the ken of legal, let alone public observers — to warp the administration of criminal justice and produce wrongful convictions" (2005: 1223). He provides examples such as docket management, plea bargaining, jury instructions, competency of counsel, prosecutorial reward structures, pre-trial procedures, and so on.

To some extent, the Mr. Big investigative scenarios straddle the concerns of second and third wave scholars of wrongful convictions. The scenarios induce confessions in a pre-arrest, pre-trial procedure that operates with few limitations. As far as we know, there are no police manuals on how to conduct these investigations, so undercover officers are forced to improvise in potentially unpredictable situations. Even though undercover officers admit that some targets falsely confess to murder (McCulloch 2008), the technique continues to be used.

In order to uncover the reasons behind wrongful convictions, supporters of the Innocence Movement have refined and expanded Hebert Packer's (1964) Crime Control and Due Process Models of criminal justice. Findley (2009), for example, describes a Reliability Model of criminal justice that relies on "best practices" and incorporates aspects of both the Crime Control and Due Process Models:

> Like the Crime Control Model, the Reliability Model emphasizes the need to efficiently and accurately sort the guilty and the innocent, and it relies more on administrative procedures than on adversarial adjudication. And the Reliability Model incorporates features of the Due Process Model, including strengthening defense counsel and the rules of evidence to force the administrative practices to respect the interests of the accused and to improve the efficiency of sorting the guilty from the innocent. (2009: 146)

According to Findley (2008: 172), the Reliability Model better protects the rights of the accused by making the fact-finding process more efficient and reliable at the administrative level, rather than relying on adversarial adjudication. Improved and more reliable investigative procedures will reduce the number of wrongfully convicted "without losing too many convictions of the guilty" (173). This sounds like a workable solution. Unfortunately, however, when the courts impose restrictions on what police officers can do in order to enhance reliability or protect the constitutional rights of the accused, the police seem to find another procedure to bypass the rules. For example, Moore, Copeland, and Schuller suggest that it is "perhaps not coincidental" that the Mr. Big technique emerged after the Supreme Court of Canada decisions in *Hebert* and *Broyles*, which restricted undercover police officers' ability to elicit confessions from in-custody suspects (2009: 349–50). Nevertheless, the Supreme Court of Canada has, in the last seventeen years, emphasized the importance of truth-finding or truth-seeking in the criminal justice system.[1]

Models are just that, models. As Packer (1964: 2) pointed out and Roach (1999: 671) reminds us, models are simplified ways of dealing with a complex criminal justice process. Roach favours multiple models because they better reflect what is happening in the criminal justice system. In fact, the right to "due process," as such, does not exist in Canadian law, although the Canadian courts do make reference to its existence in the Fifth Amendment in the United States Constitution (see, for example, *Stillman* 1997: para. 209). The equivalent terminology in Canada is the right to be tried "according to law in a fair and public hearing" (section 11(d) of the *Charter*), and not to be deprived of "life, liberty and security [except] in accordance with the principles of fundamental justice" (section 7 of the *Charter*).

Principles of fundamental justice in Canada can be found in both the *Charter* and the common law. The principle against self-incrimination (*Singh* 2007: 21) and the rule of law (*Campbell* 1999: para. 18) are two fundamental and organizing principles of the *Charter* that are relevant to Mr. Big investigations. In a free and democratic society it is important that citizens are free to remain silent in the face of police questioning (*Singh* 2007: 27) and that no one is above the law (*Campbell* 1999: para. 18).

The wrongful convictions literature identifies police-induced false confessions as one of leading causes of wrongful convictions (Drizin and Leo 2004: 918–19; Leo 2009a: 332; Macfarlane 2006: para. 249). According to the Innocence Project in the United States, 27 percent of accused who have been exonerated through DNA testing made incriminating statements or confessions at some point in their encounter with the criminal justice system (<www.innocenceproject.org>; accessed February 13, 2010). With our current knowledge that those accused who are innocent may plead guilty in court even after consulting with experienced counsel (Brockman 2010; Fitzgerald 1990), it should come as no surprise that innocent targets might confess to crimes they did not commit when subjected to a Mr. Big scenario.

As Nowlin (2004: 383) and others point out, so-called confessions in Mr. Big investigations do not have the usual characteristics of a confession — a statement against interest. These confessions have everything to do with targets trying to get themselves out of a situation where it appears to them that if they go to trial they will be convicted of a crime whether they committed it or not. A confession is in the target's best interests, not a statement against interest, as Mr. Big promises to make the nightmare (in some cases, a wrongful conviction) go away. Despite this characteristic of Mr. Big confessions, and despite the Supreme Court of Canada's acknowledgement that interrogations can produce false confessions, the Court has been reluctant to do anything about false confessions outside the narrow definition of confessions to persons in authority.

This chapter first examines the limited judicial recognition of false confessions in Canada and the move by the Supreme Court of Canada to give credence to the importance of the reliability of evidence. It then examines research that tries to illustrate how false confessions are elicited. According to Leo (2009), the road to wrongful confessions involves three sequential errors: misclassification, coercion, and contamination. This chapter then turns to these errors in light of how they might cast doubt on the reliability of confessions obtained through the Mr. Big investigative technique.

Judicial Recognition of False Confessions and the Importance of Reliability

Confession evidence has long been recognized as compelling evidence of guilt, and is considered one of the most influential and authoritative types of evidence that can be presented to a judge and/or jury (Conti 1999; Drizin and Leo 2004; Dufraimont 2008; Kassin 2008; Kassin and Gudjonsson 2004; Kassin and McNall 1991; Kassin and Neumann 1997; Kassin and Sukel 1997; Kassin and Wrightsman 1981, 1985; Leo 1992; Leo and Ofshe 1998a; Loewy 2007). According to one distinguished legal scholar, "the introduction of a confession makes the other aspects of a trial in court superfluous" (McCormick, 1972, 316). Jury simulation research shows that confessions are believed even when coerced from suspects (see Moore, Coopland, and Schuller 2009: 383–86).

The Supreme Court of Canada, in *Oickle* (2000), revisited the contemporary confessions rule and the related common law limits on police interrogation in Canada because of a "growing understanding of the problem of false confessions" (*Oickle* 2000: para. 32). In fact, the Court stated that "one of the predominant reasons" for the rule requiring confessions to be voluntary is that involuntary confessions "will often (though not always) be unreliable" (para. 47). According to Mr. Justice Iacobucci, for the majority, "the confessions rule should recognize which interrogation techniques commonly produce false confessions so as to avoid miscarriages of justice" (para. 32; discussed further in paras. 34–45).

The confessions rule has "twin goals of protecting the rights of the accused without unduly limiting society's need to investigate and solve crimes" (*Oickle*: para. 33). Mr. Justice Iacobucci described four relevant factors the trial judge should consider when determining whether a confession is voluntary: 1) threats or promises; 2) oppression; 3) the operating mind requirement; and 4) other police trickery (paras. 48–67). If an accused person's statement to a person in authority is involuntary under any of these four factors, it is inadmissible. While police trickery is concerned with voluntariness, it is also concerned with "maintaining the integrity of the criminal justice system" (para. 65) by repressing behaviour that might "shock the community" (para. 66–67). In other words, the Supreme Court of Canada endorses a due process model in its search for truth.

Legal commentators have argued that the Supreme Court of Canada's decision in *Oickle* (2000) has transformed the law so that it now sanctions police use of excessively coercive interrogation tactics (LeSage and Code 2008; Stuart 2001; Trotter 2004). LeSage and Code (2008), in particular, draw attention to the fact that these reforms have broadened the scope of admissibility of statements made by a suspect even "after repeated, lengthy and forceful interrogations, that most Crown counsel would likely not have attempted to introduce into evidence in an earlier era" (LeSage and Code 2008: 9). In 2007, the Supreme Court of Canada may have further restricted the exclusionary rule by emphasizing that "Inducements 'becom[e] improper only when... standing alone or in combination with other factors, [they] are strong enough to raise a reasonable doubt about whether the will of the subject has been overborne'" (*Spencer* 2007: para. 13, quoting *Oickle*).

Although the primary legal safeguard in Canadian criminal law is considered the confessions rule, which protects the accused against the admissibility of erroneous confessions (Sherrin 2005: para. 23; *Oickle* 2000: para. 47), under present Canadian law, involuntary confessions are excluded only if they are made to persons in authority. According to Mr. Justice Cory, for the majority in *Hodgson*, the persons in authority requirement "is carefully calibrated to ensure that the coercive power of the state is held in check and to preserve the principle against self-incrimination" (1998: para. 29; also see Penney 2004: 294). The law defines persons in authority as persons whom the confessor "reasonably believes are acting on behalf of the police or prosecuting authorities and could therefore influence or control the proceedings against him or her" (*Hodgson*: para. 48). Mr. Justice Cory specifically addressed the role of undercover police officers, stating that they "will not usually be viewed by the accused as persons in authority" (para. 48). If a suspect is unaware of the true identity of the receiver's status, then the person is not considered a person in authority for the purposes of the confessions rule (para. 39).

In *Grandinetti* (2005), the Supreme Court of Canada considered whether undercover police officers operating a Mr. Big investigation were persons in authority because they claimed to have connections with corrupt police officers. According to Madam Justice Abella, writing on behalf of the Court, the test for determining whether an individual is a person in authority is "largely subjective, focusing on the accused's perception of the person to whom he or she is making the statement"

(*Grandinetti* 2005: para. 38). She concluded that, "the state's coercive power is not engaged" when a suspect enlists the help of corrupt criminal justice officials to thwart the interests of the state (para. 44). Persons in authority are limited to "someone whom the confessor perceives to be 'an agent of the police or prosecuting authorities', 'allied with the state authorities', 'acting on behalf of the police or prosecuting authorities', and 'acting in concert with the police or prosecutorial authorities, or as their agent'" (para. 43).

Both *Hodgson* (1998) and *Grandinetti* (2005) have been criticized for limiting the voluntariness requirement to confessions made to persons in authority (Roach 2007: 213–14, 233–35). There are serious questions about whether the rule adequately protects against erroneous confessions to persons who are not considered persons in authority and against subsequent miscarriages of justice. Penney (2004: 282) suggests, "the traditional rendering of the confession rule would permit the admission of unreliable statements, for example those made in response to threats or promises by non-authorities." The Mr. Big non-custodial interrogation technique is one of those circumstances.

Anyone watching a Mr. Big scenario in action might be hard-pressed to view the undercover police officers as anything but coercive. The fact that the police officers are disguised does not render their behaviour any less so. In fact, their behaviour is more coercive, because suspects are much more likely to fear for their lives when associating with thugs than when being interrogated by police officers. Targets of Mr. Big are also more likely to confess or make up a confession because they are presented with a scenario that provides substantial rewards, but no negative consequences, for such admissions.

In examining confessions to persons in authority in *Oickle* (2000), Mr. Justice Iacobucci also recognized the dangers of using fabricated evidence when police are interrogating a suspect — "the use of false evidence is often crucial in convincing the suspect that protestations of innocence, even if true, are futile" (para. 61). He did not, however, go so far as to completely disapprove of using false evidence:

> I do not mean to suggest in any way that, standing alone, confronting the suspect with inadmissible or even fabricated evidence is necessarily grounds for excluding a statement. However, when combined with other factors, it is certainly a relevant consideration in determining on a *voir dire* whether a confession was voluntary. (para. 61)

As we will see in Chapter 3, the use of evidence (whether real, exaggerated or false) is often crucial to obtaining a confession from the target of a Mr. Big investigation. Yet these confessions are admitted into evidence without judicial scrutiny to assess their voluntariness, as is done with confessions to persons in authority. Only if defence counsel can convince the judge that the accused believed that the undercover officers were police officers will the judge then determine if the confession was voluntary. This happened in only one of the eighty-one cases we examined (*Roop* 2007). However, the judge in the end decided that Roop's confession was voluntary.

Despite recommendations by the Law Reform Commission of Canada (1984a, 1984b) and the Supreme Court of Canada's plea for reform,[2] regulation and codification of the law governing the police questioning of suspects, the area continues to be governed by the common law (Brockman and Rose 2011: 218; Bronitt 2004: 36; Sherrin 2005: para. 23). In the absence of comprehensive legislation, the judiciary has assumed a critical role, "creatively fashioning new remedies from existing evidential and procedural rules" (Bronitt 2004: 36). Yet as Sherrin (2005) points out, the courts "have merely demarcated (in fairly general terms) the outer boundaries of acceptable conduct, and have left the police to work out the best practices" (para. 23).

Canadian jurisprudence has customarily permitted the police, in their efforts to investigate crime, to engage in trickery so long as their actions do not shock the sensibilities of an informed community (*McIntyre* 1994; *Roberts* 1997; *Rothman* 1981; *Unger* 1993a). In *Mack* (1988), the Supreme Court of Canada was asked to consider the threshold limits on police misconduct in the context of entrapment, specifically, the point at which the actions of the police exceeded the permissible common law limits. Although entrapment law does not apply to Mr. Big scenarios,[3] Mr. Justice Antonio Lamer's comments (for the court) provide support for the Mr. Big technique:

> One need not be referred to evidence to acknowledge the ubiquitous nature of criminal activity in our society. If the struggle against crime is to be won, the ingenuity of criminals must be matched by that of the police; as crimes become more sophisticated so too must be the methods employed to detect their commission. (para. 15)

Mr. Justice Lamer went on to say, "Obviously the police must be given considerable latitude in the effort to enforce the standards of behaviour established in the criminal law" (para. 17). Reflecting a similar sentiment, the British Columbia Court of Appeal, in hearing an appeal from Clifford Moore, who was convicted following a Mr. Big investigation, accepted the Crown's submission that the courts "have recognized the importance of undercover techniques in the pursuit of legitimate law enforcement goals and have given the police considerable latitude in executing such strategies" (*Moore* 1997: para. 20).

The Supreme Court of Canada's endorsement of the Mr. Big operational method is buttressed by six decisions, only two of which directly addressed the admissibility of evidence from a Mr. Big operation. In *McIntyre* (1994), the Supreme Court of Canada passed up an early opportunity to assess and perhaps put an end to Mr. Big operations. Ignoring a strong dissent from the New Brunswick Court of Appeal, the Court's one-paragraph decision stated that the accused was not detained and that the "tricks used by the police were not likely to shock the community or cause the accused's statements not to be free and voluntary" (1994: para. 1). In *Grandinetti* (2005), the Court found that the undercover operators were not persons in authority even though they were claiming to have corrupt contacts in the police force that could affect the evidence. In several other Supreme Court of Canada decisions (see, for example, *Fliss* 2002; *Nett,* 2001; *O.N.E.* 2001; *Mentuck* 2001; and *Henry* 2005), the issue of the confession in a Mr. Big operation was not raised or addressed, demonstrating that the admissibility of confessions in these cases is a settled issue and the fate of Mr. Big targets is somewhat fixed. In *Osmar* (2007b), the Supreme Court of Canada refused leave to appeal, thereby rejecting an opportunity to decide whether experts should be allowed to testify about false confessions in a Mr. Big prosecution. The Ontario Court of Appeal found that the trial judge had correctly excluded the expert evidence (*Osmar* 2007a). These direct and indirect endorsements of Mr. Big investigations probably encourage police to engage in increasingly deceptive practices.

According to Mr. Justice Iacobucci, writing for six out of seven judges in the Supreme Court of Canada decision in *Oickle* (2000), "the confessions rule should recognize which interrogation techniques commonly produce false confessions so as to avoid miscarriages of justice" (para. 32). This comment and his discussion of the literature on false confessions (para. 34-45) put only a small dent in the commonsense and judicial wisdom that, generally, people do not confess to crimes they did not commit (Sherrin 2005: para. 6).

Preventing Wrongful Convictions

In *Oickle* (2000), the Supreme Court of Canada recognized that "One of the overriding concerns of the criminal justice system is that the innocent must not be convicted" (para. 36). The safeguards instituted in Canadian criminal law are thought to protect against miscarriages of justice. Typically, a wrongful conviction is the result of errors or misconduct that allows someone who is *factually* innocent to be convicted and sentenced for a crime they did not commit (Schehr and Sears 2005: 182). According to the Honourable T. Alexander Hickman (2004), all levels of the Canadian criminal justice process include a series of checks and balances designed to prevent miscarriages of justice from occurring. For instance, police investigations are reviewed internally to assess whether or not officers have complied with procedural rules; serious criminal charges are often reviewed with the Crown before the laying of an information; the accused is entitled to full and timely disclosure of all material evidence of the Crown's case; depending on the election of the accused, a preliminary inquiry will be conducted to see whether sufficient evidence exists to commit the accused to trial (although section 577 of the *Criminal Code* allows the Crown to bypass the preliminary inquiry and proceed by direct indictment); and, finally, two levels of appellate court are able to review the decisions made by lower courts (see section 675 of the *Criminal Code*) (Hickman 2004: 183–84). In British Columbia, Québec, and New Brunswick, prosecutors screen charges before they are laid by the police (Brockman and Rose 2011: 75), perhaps providing even greater protection.

Despite these checks and balances, concern about erroneous convictions and the fallibility of our adversarial criminal justice system is corroborated by the high-profile wrongful conviction cases of Donald Marshall Jr., Guy Paul Morin, Steven Truscott, David Milgaard, Wilbert Coffin, Thomas Sophonow, Clayton Johnson, Ronald Dalton, James Driskell, Gregory Parsons, William Mullins-Johnson, and Romeo Phillion — to name a few (Anderson and Anderson 2009; Campbell and Denov 2004; Denov and Campbell 2005; Macfarlane 2006; Maidment 2009; Sherrin 2005; Trotter 2004). Numerous cases have resulted in inquiries, including *The Royal Commission on the Donald Marshall, Jr. Prosecution* (Halifax: Queen's Printer, 1989); *Report of the Kaufman Commission on Proceedings Involving Guy Paul Morin* (Toronto: Ontario Ministry of the Attorney General, 1998); *The Inquiry Regarding Thomas Sophonow: The Investigation, Prosecution and Consideration of Entitlement to Compensation* (Winnipeg: Manitoba Justice, 2001); *The Lamer Commission of Inquiry Pertaining to: Ronald Dalton, Gregory Parsons and Randy Drunken: Report and Annexes* (Government of Newfoundland and Labrador, 2006); *Report of the Commission of Inquiry into the Wrongful Conviction of David Milgaard* (Saskatchewan: Office of the Attorney General, 2008); *Report of the Commission of Inquiry into Certain Aspects of the Trial and Conviction of James Driskell* (Manitoba: Office of the Attorney General, 2007); and *Inquiry into Pediatric Forensic Pathology in Ontario* (Toronto: Ontario Ministry of the Attorney General, 2008).[4]

Apart from these prominent cases, however, systematic research on wrongful conviction in Canada has historically been nominal (Anderson and Anderson 2009: 7; Brockman and Rose 2011: 144; Campbell and Denov 2004; Denov and Campbell 2005: 225). American scholars, and more recently Canadian scholars, have identified numerous factors that have contributed to erroneous convictions, including mistaken eyewitness identification, professional misconduct by criminal justice officials, misleading circumstantial evidence, erroneous forensic science, child suggestibility, the use of jailhouse informants, non-disclosure by Crown and police, unreliable expert testimony, and so on (Anderson and Anderson 2009; Bedau and Radelet 1987; Borchard 1932; Brandon and Davies 1973; Denov and Campbell 2005; Drizin and Leo 2004; Drizin and Luloff 2007; Gudjonsson 2003b; Leo 2005; Leo and Ofshe 1998a; Loewy 2007; Macfarlane 2006; Maidment 2009; Martin 2001, 2002; McMurtrie 2005; Radelet, Bedau and Putman 1992; Radin 1964; Sherrin 2005). Fewer scholars have examined the systemic extra-legal factors, such as racism, sexism, and class bias, that permeate the justice system (see Anderson and Anderson 2009 and Maidment 2009 for examples of exceptions). While the above factors are all vital to the overall understanding of wrongful convictions, this book is concerned with erroneous convictions resulting from interrogation-induced false confessions in undercover operations. Given the lack of research on such confessions, we examine the literature on in-custody interrogation and its role in inducing false confessions to see what insights it might offer into the Mr. Big operation.

According to Leo (2008: 1), police interrogations are a "microcosm for some of our most fundamental conflicts about the appropriate relationship between the state and the individual and about the norms that should guide state conduct, particularly manipulative, deceptive, and coercive conduct in the modern era." He goes on to state that such interrogations "go to the heart of our conceptions of procedural fairness and substantive justice and raise questions about the kind of criminal justice system and society we wish to have" (2008: 1).

The Extent of False Confessions

Notwithstanding the fact that the incidence of interrogation-induced false confessions is difficult to estimate (Cassell 1998), Drizin and Leo (2004) suggest that the hundreds of cases that have been discovered and documented to date "understate the true nature and extent of the phenomenon" (919), and likely represent only the tip of the iceberg (Anderson and Anderson 2009: 7; Drizin and Leo 2004: 919; Ofshe and Leo 1997a: 191). What is currently known about the phenomenon of false confessions has come from statistical analysis of archival and documentary records (Bedau and Radelet 1987; Leo and Ofshe 1998a; Warden 2003; Drizin and Leo 2004; Gross et al. 2005), experimental psychological research (Breau and Brook 2007; Kassin and Neumann 1997; Kassin and Sukel 1997; Redlich and Goodman 2003), self-report interviews and surveys (Gudjonsson and Petursson 1991; Gudjonsson and Sigurdsson 1999), and naturalistic observation (Gudjonsson, Clare, Rutter, and Pearse 1993; Leo 1996a, 1996b, 1996c). These studies have shown that interrogator-induced false confessions have become or are becoming one of the more prominent and enduring causes of wrongful conviction (Leo and Ofshe 1998a; Drizin and Leo 2004; Leo 2007; Warden 2003).

According to Drizin and Leo (2004), police-induced false confessions occur in 14 percent to 25 percent of documented wrongful convictions (906). Moreover, researchers have consistently found that false confessions are concentrated in the most serious indictable offences, and are a leading source of error in wrongful homicide convictions (Drizin and Leo 2004; Gross 1996; Leo 2007; Macfarlane 2006; Meissner and Russano 2003). It may be that those convicted of less serious offences as a result of false confessions or false guilty pleas cannot be bothered to engage the justice system to reverse their wrongful convictions. It may also be the case that police officers put less effort into the less serious crimes, and that there are fewer false confessions with such crimes.

A 1932 watershed study conducted by Yale University law professor Edwin Borchard is believed to be the first systematic study on miscarriages of justice (Drizin and Leo 2004: 900; Gudjonsson 2003b: 159; Harmon 2001: 951; Leo 2005: 203; Macfarlane 2006: para. 14). Following it, a series of books documenting various other alleged or proven cases of miscarriages of justice emerged, emphasizing that wrongful convictions do occur and documenting newer cases (Drizin and Leo 2004: 901).[5] Although useful, these earlier studies were based on anecdotal and descriptive accounts rather than rigorous scientific methods (Gudjonsson 2003b: 159). No systematic, scientific studies documenting the causes, patterns, implications, and consequences of miscarriages of justice emerged until the late 1980s (Drizin and Leo 2004: 902).

Bedau and Radelet's (1987) groundbreaking article, "Miscarriages of Justice in Potentially Capital Cases," dispelled the common perception that factually innocent persons would not implicate themselves in crimes they did not commit. In their analysis of 350 cases in which individuals were wrongfully convicted of capital or potentially capital crimes in the U.S. from 1900 to 1987, Bedau and Radelet (1987) discovered that interrogation-induced false confessions played a causal role in 49 (11.4 percent) of the 350 instances of miscarriages of justice (57).[6] In the years after the Bedau-Radelet study, scientific and technological developments in DNA testing and its application to post-conviction cases led to a surge of proven miscarriages of justice (Drizin and Leo 2004: 903; Drizin and Luloff 2007: 257; Garrett 2008: 56; McMurtrie 2005: 1271). This prompted the social scientific investigation into miscarriages of justice, which gained even more momentum through the 1990s.

Leo and Ofshe (1998a) reviewed a sample of sixty cases of wrongful conviction resulting from alleged police-induced false confession throughout the United States, between 1973 and 1996.[7] Notably, there was no significant and/or credible evidence to corroborate the suspects' impugned confessional statements, and evidence supporting their factual innocence was "often substantial and compelling" (436). Based on the strength of the evidence against the accused, false confessions were classified into three categories: proven, highly probable, and probable false confessions (436–37). Based on this classification system, 34 (57 percent) were categorized as "proven false confessions," 18 (30 percent) were "highly probable," and 8 (13 percent) were classified as "probable false confessions" (Leo and Ofshe 1998a: 444–49). What sets this study apart from other research on wrongful conviction is that it is the first to focus specifically on miscarriages of justice caused by police-induced false confessions (Leo and Ofshe 1998b: 433–34). It is worth noting that 27 percent of the false confessors in this study were intellectually disadvantaged (213–14).

Warden (2003) analyzed the role of false confessions in known erroneous murder convictions in Illinois since 1970. Of the 42 cases examined, he found that twenty-five defendants (60 percent) confessed falsely. In other words, false confessions were the leading cause of wrongful conviction in the Illinois homicide cases studied. Had investigators diligently pursued information acquired in the early stages of their investigations, thirteen (52 percent) of the wrongful convictions might have been avoided. One quarter may have been averted had defendants received effective assistance of counsel (Warden 2003).

In 2004, Drizin and Leo published an unparalleled study entitled "The Problem of False Confessions In the Post-DNA World," in which they analyzed a total of 125 cases of proven false confessions in the United States between 1971 and 2002.[8] To avoid duplication, the authors excluded from their sample the thirty-four proven false confession cases unearthed by Leo and Ofshe (1998a). In line with previous wrongful conviction research, an overwhelming number of false confessions occurred in more serious indictable offences, murder being the largest category (81 percent), distantly followed by rape (9 percent) and arson (3 percent) (Drizin and Leo 2004: 944).

Results indicate that age and mental capacity are two vulnerability factors that increase the likelihood of suspects falsely confessing to a crime they did not commit. One of the more troubling findings with respect to age was that suspects under the age of eighteen accounted for forty false confessions (35 percent of the sample). Moreover, seven children under the age of fourteen gave false confessions during an interrogation (961). These findings suggest a correlation between age and the likelihood of eliciting a false confession (942). Drizin and Leo (2004) also found that intellectually disadvantaged persons were particularly vulnerable to falsely confessing when subjected to modern psychological interrogation techniques, identifying at least twenty-seven (22 percent) intellectually disadvantaged defendants in their sample of false confessors.

A Canadian study involving a survey of convicted men suggests that "false confessions might be more likely to occur with more vulnerable individuals, that is, suspects with no prior experience with the criminal justice system, who lack social support as well as those not invoking their legal right to consult a lawyer" (Deslauriers-Varin, Lussier, and St-Yves 2009: 30). Notwithstanding the fact that individuals who suffer from cognitive deficits are disproportionately represented in false confession cases, Drizin and Leo (2004) report that an overwhelming number "of reported false confessions are from cognitively and intellectually normal individuals" (918). To date, the Drizin and Leo study contains the largest catalogue of cases that focus specifically on the phenomenon of (proven) interrogation-induced false confession.

More recently, Gross et al. (2005) identified a comprehensive catalogue of 340 exonerations of persons wrongfully convicted from 1989 to 2003. Significantly, fifty-one (15 percent) of the 340 erroneous convictions involved defendants who confessed to crimes they did not commit (544). Police coercion was seen as the cause of false confessions in twenty-eight (55 percent) cases, while five (10 percent) were volunteered. Akin to the study conducted by Drizin and Leo (2004), Gross et al. (2005) found that the most vulnerable groups of innocent defendants included youth and those with mental disabilities. At the time of their confession, thirty-three false confessors were under the age of eighteen. Astonishingly, nine of the juvenile exonerees were aged twelve to fifteen (545). False confessions were even more frequent among those with mental disabilities. Of the twenty-six persons who suffered from intellectual deficits and mental illness, eighteen (69 percent) of them falsely confessed (545). As a final note, both Drizin and Leo (2004) and Gross et al. (2005) found that at least 80 percent of the police-induced false confessions occurred in homicide cases and other high-profile felonies (Leo 2007: 33).[9]

Until recent years, those who were wrongfully convicted were, according to Warden (2003: 1), considered to be "regrettable anomalies in an otherwise well-functioning criminal justice system" (see also Anderson and Anderson 2009: 7). These studies, however, suggest that police-induced false confessions, and subsequent miscarriages of justice, are not as infrequent as once thought; instead, they occur with regular and disconcerting frequency (Denov and Campbell 2005; Drizin and Leo 2004; Gudjonsson 2003b; Leo 2007 and 2008; Leo and Ofshe 1998a; Sherrin 2005).

Causes of False Confessions

Given the fact that "third-degree" interrogation tactics "have faded into the annals of criminal justice history" (Kassin and Gudjonsson 2004: 41) and have been replaced with more subtle forms of manipulation, deception, and coercion, it is no wonder that false confessions might be thought of today as unlikely and rare (Ofshe and Leo 1997b: 983). Why factually innocent persons continue to implicate themselves in crimes they have not committed (high-profile murders at that) is one of the more perplexing questions social science research has attempted to answer. According to Gudjonsson's (2003a: 165) Interaction Model, there are numerous different causes, or different combinations of factors, that must be considered when evaluating cases of disputed confessions, and "each case must be considered on its own merit" (see also Gudjonsson 2003b: 193).[10] Leo (2009) suggests that the process of false confessions starts with misclassification.

The Misclassification Error

In any investigation, the police first have to decide whom to target. Numerous academics and government officials have written about the horrific consequences of tunnel vision and confirmation and cognitive biases (Burke 2006; Findley and Scott 2006; Kersholt and Eikelboom 2006; Leo and Davis 2009; Martin 2002), while others address police misconduct or mishandling of investigations in terms of whom they target and how they go about targeting individuals who are later exonerated (Bellemare and Finlayson 2004; Leo 2009; MacFarlane 2006). Anderson and Anderson (2009) and Maidment (2009) point to factors such as race and socio-economic status that might also direct tunnel vision.

MacFarlane (2006, 2008) outlines some of the circumstances that might predispose police to pursue the wrong track early in their investigation: 1) public and media pressure to solve the crime quickly; 2) the existence of an unpopular target; 3) conversion of the adversarial process into a game where prosecutors lose sight of their goal and set out to secure a conviction; and 4) noble cause corruption in the police force — "where police believe that it is justifiable to fabricate or artificially improve evidence, or in some other fashion bend the rules, to secure the conviction of someone they are satisfied is guilty" (2006: para. 135). Once a person is targeted, whether the person committed the crime or not, the Mr. Big scenario is quite successful in obtaining a confession. In sometimes extremely frightful scenarios, which may compel them to plead guilty to crimes they did not commit, targets are presented with irresistible financial and other incentives and confronted with real or fabricated evidence implicating them in crimes.

The truth of confessions cannot be established by police confidence that they are interrogating or targeting the right person. This might seem rather obvious, but in 2004, when Joseph Buckley, president of an organization that has trained tens of thousands of law-enforcement personnel, was asked if "his persuasive methods did not at times cause innocent people to confess," he responded, "No, because we don't interrogate innocent people" (quoted in Kassin and Gudjonsson 2004: 36). Leo (2009: 334) suggests that detectives are misleadingly taught that they can distinguish true from false statements when in fact their training often makes them less reliable as predictors of truth-telling.

The Coercion Error

The second step in false confessions, according to Leo (2009: 334), is the coercion error. To fully grasp the complexity of this phenomenon, researchers have focused on two primary sources: modern psychological interrogation methods used by the interrogator and the psychological vulnerabilities of persons being questioned (Meissner and Russano 2003; Sherrin 2005: para. 43).

Although still in its infancy, the scientific research on interrogation and confession points to police over-zealousness, poor training, and negligence as the principal causes of most false confessions (Anderson and Anderson 2009: 10–11; Bedau and Radelet 1987; Drizin and Leo 2004: 917; Kennedy 1986; Ofshe and Leo 1997b: 983; Redlich and Goodman 2003: 143). Misdirected police training and negligence are perpetuated by authors of leading interrogation manuals[11] and police trainers, who, despite empirical research on interrogation and confession, argue that contemporary psychological interrogation methods do not lead innocent persons to confess to crimes they did not commit (Findley and Scott 2006: 333; Gohara 2006: 841; Gudjonsson 2003b: 9; Leo 2007: 33; Leo 2009; Leo and Ofshe 1998a: 492; Ofshe and Leo 1997b: 983; Sherrin 2005: para. 23; White 1997: 108). It has even been suggested that "the more training that police get in interrogation techniques, the less likely they are to be aware of their possible fallibility" (Meyer and Reppucci 2007: 776).

By its very nature, interrogation is a guilt-presumptive process, defined by Kassin and Gudjonsson (2004) as "a theory-driven social interaction led by an authority figure who holds a strong a priori belief about the target and who measures success by the ability to extract an admission from that target" (41). Interrogation tactics create a "sequential influence process" (Ofshe and Leo 1997a: 194), a cost/

benefit analysis whereby suspects evaluate the potential courses of action available, the relative short- and long-term consequences attached to each of the options available to them, and the utility of value benefits, corresponding harms or gains attached to prospective courses of action (Drizin and Leo 2004: 912; Gudjonsson 2003b: 121; Ofshe and Leo 1997b: 985–86). According to Gudjonsson (2003b), the decision to confess is governed by the "*subjective probabilities of occurrence of the perceived consequences*" (121) — that is to say, the suspect's choices and behaviours are guided not by objective or even realistic consequences, but by what he/she subjectively believes might happen. Therefore it follows that if police officers (or undercover police officers) box suspects into a corner where the only way out is to confess, a confession will often be forthcoming.

Gudjonsson and Clark (1986) propose the concept of interrogative suggestibility to help account for individual differences in the way suspects respond to the pressures of police interrogation and custodial confinement. Interrogative suggestibility is defined as "the extent to which, within a closed social interaction, people come to accept messages communicated during formal questioning, as the result of which their subsequent behavioural response is affected" (84).[12] The theory postulates that an individual's susceptibility to an interrogator's suggestions will depend on his or her cognitive processing capacity, or the coping strategies he or she is able to generate and implement when faced with the conditions of uncertainty, interpersonal trust, and heightened expectations (Gudjonsson 2003b: 348–50).

Ofshe and Leo (1997b) and Drizin and Leo (2004) suggest that there are two ways to obtain a false confession from innocent suspects. The first is to lead suspects to believe that their circumstances are so unjust and hopeless that only a confession will improve their situation. The second is to convince suspects that they probably committed the crime but have no recollection or memory of it and that confessing is the best course of action (Drizin and Leo 2004: 913). The two-step interrogation process involves psychological manipulation: the suspect loses confidence and is convinced that he or she is powerless in light of "seemingly objective and incontrovertible evidence of his guilt, whether or not any actually exists" (2004: 913). Such evidence may be fabricated, exaggerated, or real. The interrogator continues to convey the message that resistance is futile (914). The second step is to elicit the confession through various tactics, including low-end inducements (such as an appeal to morality), systemic inducements (admissions will result in more favourable treatment by the criminal justice system), and high-end inducements (admissions will result in a lighter penalty) (2004: 914–15)

As indicated above, some individuals are at increased risk to give false self-incriminating statements while in police custody due to psychological factors such as diminished cognitive functioning (low I.Q., poor memory capacity), mental disorders (mental illness, learning disability, personality disorder), personality traits (suggestibility, compliance, acquiescence) and abnormal mental states (anxiety, phobic problems such as claustrophobia, depression, post-traumatic stress disorder, drug or alcohol intoxication or withdrawal symptoms) (Gudjonsson 2003b, 316–20). A review of the extant psychological literature indicates that false confessions are most acute among adolescents and individuals believed to be suffering from developmental disabilities (i.e., learning or intellectual deficits, mental illness), owing to the fact that these two subgroups are more suggestible and/or compliant, and typically lack the psychological resources necessary to resist the overwhelming pressures of interrogation (Drizin and Leo 2004: 907; Gudjonsson 2003b: 621; Gudjonsson and Henry 2003; Kassin 1997: 221–28; Medford, Gudjonsson, and Pearse 2003; Ofshe and Leo 1997b: 1117; Redlich and Goodman 2003: 143).

The Contamination Error

According to Leo (2009: 337), a mere "I did it" is not the end of the confession. In the post-admission narrative, the police help the suspect develop a compelling story that makes the confession more believable. The story lines may be why confessions are "treated as such powerful evidence of guilt and sometimes lead to the prosecution and conviction of the innocent" (2009: 337). If in-custody interrogations are videotaped in their entirety, interrogator contamination may be deciphered (2009: 337). However, in the Mr. Big investigation, much of the grooming of the target may take place prior to wiretap authorization, and is therefore unrecorded. If contamination of evidence has occurred at this early stage in the investigation, there will be no record of it.

A Typology of False Confessions

The diverse psychological reasons why people confess to crimes they did not commit lead the continuing discourse about the most suitable method to categorize the various types of false confessions. There are three prominent models put forth to explain why individuals succumb to the psychological pressures of interrogation. The most widely cited taxonomy is the Kassin-Wrightsman (1985) model, which is based on anecdotal evidence and psychological theories of attitude change (Gudjonsson 2003b: 194). According to this framework, false confessions are classified into three psychologically distinct types: voluntary, coerced-compliant, and coerced-internalized (Kassin 2008: 195),[13] although some researchers do not use "coerced" in the last two types (Leo 2009: 338). A voluntary false confession is one in which a suspect, devoid of police pressures (i.e., physical and/or psychological coercion), spontaneously offers a self-incriminating statement for a crime he or she did not commit (Kassin 2008: 195). Such confessions are often the result of an underlying psychological problem, but may also result from other reasons such as protecting the real criminal (Leo 2009: 338). A coerced-compliant confession results when an individual acquiesces to escape the enduring, stressful, or intolerable pressures of the interrogation process "for some immediate instrumental gain" (Gudjonsson 2003b: 196).[14] The coerced-internalized false confession occurs when an individual, "subjected to highly suggestive methods of interrogation"

(Kassin 1997: 226), is persuaded that he/she has in fact committed a crime but has no recollection of having committed it (Gudjonsson 2003b: 196; Ofshe and Leo 1997a: 208).[15]

Although Kassin and Wrightsman have unquestionably contributed to a better understanding of the nature of false confessions, this threefold typology is not without flaws. Significantly, not all compliant and internalized false confessions are coerced (Gudjonsson 2003b: 201). Moreover, this model does not allow for certain types of confessions to be classified (e.g., someone who confesses to protect someone else).[16] The most effective way to overcome this flaw is to increase the number of categories, which is precisely what Ofshe and Leo (1997a) do with their alternative classification system. In order to distinguish between confessions caused by police coercion and those caused by stress experienced by the suspect being interrogated, Ofshe and Leo (1997a) created the *stress-compliant* and *coerced-compliant* false confessions categories (Sherrin 2005: para. 33).[17] One of the limitations of the Ofshe-Leo model, however, is that it focuses largely on police interrogative pressure and interrogator-induced false confessions while ignoring factors such as the custodial environment itself, coercion from an external source (e.g., a spouse, family member, friend), and psychological vulnerabilities (i.e., low I.Q., high suggestibility and compliance, anxiety and phobic disorders, and personality disorder) (Gudjonsson 2003b: 206). The Kassin and Wrightsman (1985) conceptual model also fails to address the police interrogative pressures and inducements found in non-custodial environments.

In a modified framework, Gudjonsson (2003b) retains the Kassin–Wrightsman threefold typology but replaces the term *coerced* with *pressured* because it is a more inclusive term that encompasses most types of false confessions. Gudjonsson classifies confessions as *voluntary, pressured-internalized,* or *pressured-compliant* (211); that is to say, the model classifies the source of pressure placed upon the person being interrogated. As evidenced in the Kassin-Wrightsman model, not all compliant and internalized false confessions are coerced; some may be a result of external pressures independent of police influence (Gudjonsson 2003b: 201). The source of pressure is categorized as *internal* (psychological need to confess), *custodial* (coming from the police or other agencies granted with arrest/detention powers), or *non-custodial* (coming from persons other than the police or officers acting in an undercover capacity) (Gudjonsson 2003b: 212). However, Gudjonsson (2003b) cautions that classifying false confessions into psychologically distinct categories may not always be possible, since elements from the three categories may overlap and, thus, are not exclusive (242).

Mr. Big and False Confessions

Perhaps the greatest advantage of Gudjonsson's modified framework is that it recognizes non-custodial settings as a source of pressure. As alluded to in the introduction, Gudjonsson (2003b) conducted a lengthy, comprehensive analysis of the case involving Andrew Rose, and concluded that Rose's confession "was a pressured-compliant type of confession" which was likely false (581). The confession was coerced by undercover police officers purporting to be criminal figures in an elaborate criminal syndicate (581). Gudjonsson (2003b) explains:

> They encouraged Rose to participate in apparent criminal activities of that organization, psychologically manipulated his perception of the likely outcome in his forthcoming trial, played on his vulnerabilities and distress concerning his case and used threats and inducements to break down his persistent claims of innocence. The immense pressure that Rose was placed under, and the extreme distress he displayed during the three videotaped interviews, raises important ethical issues about the use of non-custodial interrogations in a case like this. (581)

While there are variations in the Mr. Big scenarios, the thrust of the covert technique remains the same: undercover police officers adopt fictional criminal identities, posing as members of an authentic, criminal syndicate, with the overall aim of eliciting incriminating statements from the target of their investigation.

Though successful in achieving its desired result, the Mr. Big strategy has provoked a storm of protest from scholars and members of the legal community alike. Many argue that these role-playing scenarios undermine the fundamental principles of justice, exceed professional and ethical boundaries, and are a catalyst for eliciting false confessions (Gudjonsson 2003b; Hutchinson 2004; Leo 1992; Libin 2009; Moore, Copeland, and Schuller 2009; Mulgrew 2005; Nowlin 2004; Smith, Stinson, and Patry 2009). Pundits say the self-incriminating statements are invariably induced by promises of wealth and professional advancement in a sophisticated criminal organization, not to mention avoidance of criminal sanctions by having the organization make the consequences of the crime disappear. Targets might not only intentionally overestimate their participation and culpability in the crime under investigation, but also distort or fabricate stories of previous misdeeds to portray themselves as worthy candidates to join a wealthy criminal organization or to protect their own safety (*Henry* 2003: para. 44). Critics contend that these circumstances gravely undermine the reliability of confessions and could increase the chances that innocent persons might confess to crimes they did not commit.

Christopher Nowlin, an academic and practicing criminal defence lawyer, analyzed four cases involving a confession obtained from a Mr. Big operation. He concluded that these post-offence undercover operations tend to produce unreliable, and at times "patently false," confessions (2004: 394). Since targets do not fully appreciate the potential consequences of confessing, statements made in the context of a Mr. Big sting are not statements against the target's penal interest but rather are made in anticipation that the crime boss can make criminal problems go away (413).

Prominent defence lawyer James Lockyer opposes deceptive interrogations conducted in the Mr. Big operations because the resulting confessions would require substantial extrinsic support to be considered reliable. Such support is rare (Hutchinson 2004: RB1; Mulgrew 2005: B1). Defence lawyer Daniel Brodsky, a member of the Association in Defence of the Wrongly Convicted (AIDWYC), says that it is customary for juries to convict accused persons subjected to Mr. Big scenarios because they accept the widespread, intuitive notion that innocent persons would not implicate themselves in crimes they did not commit (Staples 2007: A13). Although most people find it difficult to believe that anyone would confess to a crime they have not committed, research indicates that the phenomenon of false confessions occurs with regular and disconcerting frequency (Bedau and Radelet 1987; Drizin and Leo 2004; Gross, Jacoby, Matheson, Montgomery, and Patil 2005; Leo and Ofshe 1998a; Scheck, Neufeld, and Dwyer 2000; Warden 2003). Notwithstanding this wealth of empirical evidence, this "psychological myth of interrogation" continues to dominate attitudes not only among the general populace but also among criminal justice officials (Drizin and Leo 2004; Johnson 1997; Kassin 1997, Kassin and Neumann 1997; Kassin and Wrightsman 1980, 1981; Leo 2007; Ofshe and Leo 1997b). A closer examination of Mr. Big cases in Chapter 3 illustrates how the police obtain confessions and the factors that may make them unreliable.

Notes

1. A search of the Supreme Court of Canada database through Quicklaw turns up twenty-nine criminal decisions, most very recent, but beginning in 1993, which use the term "truth-seeking." Some of these decisions are discussed later in this book. The terms "reliability" and "reliable" are used more frequently.
2. In *Hodgson* (1998), Cory for the majority wrote, "The unfairness of admitting statements coerced by private individuals should be recognized. However, it is the sort of change which should be studied by Parliament and remedied by enactment.... Because of the very real possibility of a resulting miscarriage of justice and the fundamental unfairness of admitting statements coerced by the violence of private individuals, I would hope that the study will not be long postponed" (para. 29).
3. Mr. Big investigations do not involve entrapment, as they are post-offence undercover operations to elicit confessions. In other words, the police have not instigated the offence but are attempting to apprehend the perpetrator of a crime that has already been committed. There were, however, a couple of Mr. Big cases where the police also instigated an offence.
4. Maidment (2009: 111) provides a summary table of the length, cost, and other factors associated with six of these inquiries.
5. See Brandon and Davies (1973), Frank and Frank (1957), Gardner (1952), and Radin (1964).
6. According to Bedau and Radelet (1987), a miscarriage of justice occurred in cases where "(a) The defendant was convicted of homicide or sentenced to death for rape; and (b) when either (i) no such crime actually occurred, or (ii) the defendant was legally and physically uninvolved in the crime" (45).
7. Criteria for inclusion in the study included: 1) the confession was coerced by police;

2) the confession statement formed the basis of the state's case against the accused; 3) the confession was not supported by any physical or reliable inculpatory evidence; and 4) other evidence, often substantial and compelling, factually supported the defendant's innocence (436).

8. All 125 cases were categorized as proven because at least one piece of evidence positively established the suspect's innocence beyond a reasonable doubt (Drizin and Leo 2004: 928). Significantly, Drizin and Leo (2004) identified two recurrent sources that led to the exoneration of the factually innocent: scientific evidence (46 percent) and the identification of the real perpetrator (74 percent) (953–54).

9. False confessions are likely to occur in more serious cases because of increased public and institutional pressures to resolve these crimes (Gross 1996: 478; Leo 2007: 32; Macfarlane 2006: para. 121). While true, this statement might nevertheless ignore the number of wrongful convictions obtained through efficiency and plea-bargaining (see Brockman 2010 and Brockman and Rose 2011: 79–80).

10. Various factors include custodial pressures, interrogation techniques, behaviour of the interrogator, personal vulnerabilities of the suspect, and presence or absence of legal counsel.

11. According to Gudjonsson (2003b), both the Inbau, Reid, and Buckley (1986) and the Inbau, Reid, Buckley, and Jayne (2001) texts have influenced numerous other interrogation manual authors.

12. Gudjonsson (2003b) argues that this definition "provides the framework for a theoretical model that helps to further our understanding of the process and outcome of the police interview" (346). His definition of interrogative suggestibility is all-encompassing, taking into account five components of the interrogative process: social interaction; questioning procedure; a suggestive stimulus; acceptance of the stimulus; and a behavioural response to that stimulus (346).

13. See Kassin and Wrightsman (1985) for a detailed explanation of these three types of confession (76–78).

14. A form of social influence, compliance is "conformity that involves publicly acting in accord with social pressure while privately disagreeing" (Myers and Spencer 2001: 210) and is done for instrumental purposes (gain reward or avoid punishment). This type of public capitulation can be traced to Asch's (1956) studies of conformity (group pressure) and Milgram's (1974) research on obedience to authority (Kassin 1997: 225). This phenomenon is illustrated in the 1692 Salem witch trials, *Brown v. Mississippi* 297 U.S. 278 No. 301 (1936), and the infamous Central Park jogger case (Drizin and Leo 2004; Gudjonsson 2003b; Russano, Meissner, Narchet, and Kassin 2005).

15. A deeper form of social influence, internalization "refers to a private acceptance of the beliefs espoused by others" (Kassin 1997: 225), and is exemplified in Sherif's (1936) autokinetic studies on the formation of group norms (Kassin 1997: 225; Myers and Spencer 2001: 211–13).

16. For an in-depth evaluation of the Kassin-Wrightsman model, see Gudjonsson 2003b: 201–03 and Ofshe and Leo 1997a: 209.

17. For a more thorough explanation of the Ofshe-Leo classification system, see Ofshe and Leo 1997a: 210–20.

3

Contacting and Grooming the Target to Elicit Confessions

This chapter first presents some of the characteristics of Mr. Big operations before describing the methods used to contact and groom the targets in preparation for eliciting a confession from them.

Demographic and Other Descriptive Data

Of the ninety-three accused in these eighty-one cases, eighty-nine were men and four were women.[1] Two of the targets were juveniles, defined by the *Youth Criminal Justice Act* as persons under the age of eighteen. The age of the remaining accused ranged from nineteen to fifty-nine years of age.[2]

Although the information was not available for all targets, we established that eleven of the targets were Aboriginal and at least twenty-nine came from economically disadvantaged backgrounds. For example, Nelson Hart, who "had a grade four education and a history of seizures," came from a "lifetime of welfare and poverty" (Moore, Copeland, and Schuller 2009: 354, 356). Walter Anderson's financial circumstances were "precarious," and the undercover operatives offered him "money to carry out various illicit activities" (para. 11). C.K.R.S. was so desperate for money and a job that he offered to kill an undercover officer for between $20 and $25,000 (para. 83). He was led to believe that he would receive "a major payoff of $30,000" for his work for Mr. Big and that it would lead to "a real job, that would give him real money" (para. 84). Wesley Evans was so desperate for friends, the undercover police officers said, that he followed them like a "puppy dog." In addition, he "had barely enough money to survive at a subsistence level. The undercover operators bought him liquor, gave him money to buy drugs and shoes and bought him food" (para. 14). The list of desperate financial circumstances goes on and on (further examples are discussed below under "Money as a Significant Grooming Tool").

Table 1 presents the geographic location of the court proceedings in this study. Consistent with reports that the technique originated in British Columbia, fifty-six of the eighty-one cases examined were heard in that province. Of the other cases, seven were heard in Alberta, fives in Manitoba, four in Ontario, three in Saskatchewan, two in each of Newfoundland and Québec, and one in each of New Brunswick and Nova Scotia.

In *Dix* (2001), Sergeant Greg Smith, in charge of Undercover Coordination for the "K" Division of the RCMP (Edmonton, Alberta), testified that these undercover operations are "often used as a last resort technique in homicide investigations. They are inherently dangerous and are reserved for the most serious criminal offences"

Table 1: Geographic Location of Offence/Court Proceedings

Province	Frequency	Percentage
British Columbia	56	69.1 percent
Alberta	7	8.6 percent
Saskatchewan	3	3.7 percent
Manitoba	5	6.2 percent
Ontario	4	4.9 percent
Québec	2	2.5 percent
New Brunswick	1	1.2 percent
Nova Scotia	1	1.2 percent
Newfoundland	2	2.5 percent
Total	81	100 percent

(para. 14). The results show nothing to refute the claim that the police resort to this technique when traditional investigative procedures have proven ineffective and unsuccessful. There was support for this claim in 46 cases.

The average time lapse between the commission of the offence and the commencement of the undercover operation was 46.3 months (the median was fifteen months). In all but four cases, the Mr. Big technique was used to investigate unsolved homicides. In *Carter* (2001), the accused was charged with conspiracy to commit murder, counselling murder, and attempted murder. In *Joseph* (2000a), both co-accused were charged with two counts of attempted murder and other offences involving firearms and aggravated assault (para. 1–2). The accused in *Steadman* (2008) was charged with being an accessory after the fact to murder, and obstructing a peace officer in the course of an investigation into that murder (para. 1). And as a result of the Mr. Big investigation targeting Steven Ryan Porsch, the accused was charged with ten counts including four charges of counseling to commit arson, assault causing bodily harm, robbery, and a number of firearm offences (*Porsch* 2007: para. 1).

Since murder is a serious indictable offence (section 469 of the *Criminal Code*), the accused must be tried in a superior court of criminal jurisdiction by judge and jury (section 471). There is one exception: an accused may be tried by a superior court judge without a jury, provided both the accused and the Attorney General consent (section 473). Of the ninety-three accused persons, sixteen pleaded guilty. Of the seventy-seven remaining, sixty-one (79 percent) were tried by judge and jury, and sixteen (21 percent) by judge alone. Alas, none of the sixteen cases indicates why the accused and the Crown agreed to a trial by judge alone. However, one could reasonably speculate that the accused wished to avoid a jury because the admission of the undercover operation narrative (the circumstances surrounding the confession), would in its unedited entirety, have provided evidence suggesting the accused's bad character or criminal disposition. Such evidence has been shown to have a highly prejudicial effect on juries, despite trial judges' instructions not to use the evidence for such a purpose (Sopinka, Lederman, and Bryant 1999: 471; also see Nowlin 2005, 2006). Character evidence and its admissibility are discussed in greater detail below.

Given the inherently prejudicial nature of the post-offence undercover operation, the accused might have a better chance of acquittal if tried by a superior court judge alone.[3] Table 2 shows that a finding of guilt is more likely when the accused person chose a trial by judge and jury. Of those accused tried by judge and jury, 90 percent were convicted, compared to only 69 percent of accused tried by judge alone.

The RCMP website states that 95 percent of the Mr. Big cases that are prosecuted result in a conviction (RCMP 2009). As Table 2 indicates, a guilty verdict was reached in sixty-six cases, while a guilty plea was entered in sixteen cases, bringing the total guilty verdicts to eighty-two, or an 88 percent conviction rate. The somewhat lower figure in this study than that in the police report could be attributed to a larger number of negotiated guilty pleas (see Brockman and Rose 2011: 79–80) that did not appear in the legal databases. Though it was not stated why sixteen of the accused pleaded guilty, one could infer that a guilty plea was the result of either an overwhelming body of evidence against the accused, or an effort to avoid an anticipated harsher sentence following a trial (Anderson and Anderson 2009: 20).

It has become apparent that the use of evidence from Mr. Big operations is not limited to the accused who stand trial, but may also extend to witnesses. In *Ferber* (2000), a witness who was the subject of a Mr. Big operation refused to testify at the accused's trial because he feared that "he, his wife and baby son were all at grave physical risk if he testified" (para. 21). A *voir dire* was held to determine if his statements (some of which were made during the undercover operation) were admissible under an exception to the hearsay rule as "KGB statements." The trial judge excluded them, commenting, "This Court is not of the view [that] K.G.B. authorizes the use of this kind of hearsay against accused persons without the protection of cross-examination" (para. 76). A similar event happened in *Sihota*

Table 2: Verdicts of Trials by Judge and Jury, and by Judge Alone

		Trial by		Total
		Judge and Jury	Judge Alone	
Judgment	Guilty	55 (90 percent)	11 (69 percent)	66
	Not guilty	6 (10 percent)	5 (31 percent)	11
Total[4]		61 (100 percent)	16 (100 percent)	77

(2009 paras. 7–9), where a witness had been part of a Mr. Big operation. He was subjected to cross-examination, but his evidence was given little weight. Though not included in our database, these cases illustrate the net-widening or "creep-effect" of Mr. Big scenarios.

Methods of Initiating Contact with the Target

The intention of the first operational scenario is to make contact with the target, in an attempt to establish the operative's credibility as a member of a sophisticated criminal syndicate and to befriend the target in the hopes of forming a relationship that could result in the target's disclosing inculpatory statements that would advance the investigation (Baron 2008a: A4; *Cretney* 1999: para. 10). During the first "accidental" meeting, the operative is often in need of assistance and aims to enlist the help of the targeted suspect. There are six recurring methods of initiating contact with the suspect that emerged from the analysis: 1) the operative meets the target in police custody; 2) the target is informed that he or she is a "grand prize winner" in a contest; 3) the operative and target meet at the suspect's place of employment/school; 4) the undercover officers stage a breakdown of their vehicle; 5) the police use a third party; and 6) contact is made with the target in a drinking establishment.

Police Custody

Recruiting suspects while in custody was one of the most prevalent of tactics, occurring in ten cases. In *T.C.M.* (2007), the target, a youth at the time, was one of many alleged to have been involved in a fatal shooting in front of the Argyll Hotel in Vancouver, British Columbia (para. 6). The operation began when police officers arrested T.C.M. and placed him in a police wagon and then a holding cell with an

Figure 1: Methods of Initiating Contact with the Target

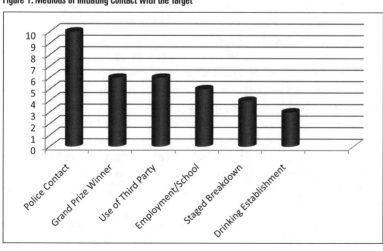

undercover operative, who impersonated a wealthy criminal "engaged in money-laundering and other high-level financial or similar crimes" (para. 12). Following his release from custody, the operative informed the target of potential employment opportunities with the organization (para. 12). T.C.M. was paid for various tasks and told he could expect to earn more money. He "began to see a very real possibility of moving to a much better life, from his existence as a small-time drug dealer 'working the Block' for long and late hours on the streets of the downtown eastside" (para. 13). T.C.M. would be taken in by the undercover ruse and would participate in several scenarios before confessing to the crime (para. 13).

In order to win the trust of George Clayton Mentuck (featured in Chapter 1), the RCMP hired Douglas Brau, a prisoner at Brandon Correctional Institute at the same time as Mentuck, to act as an informant and aide to the operation (Mentuck 2000b: para. 74). He visited the accused four times prior to his release and was tasked with selling Mentuck on the possibility of working with Mr. Brau in a criminal organization following his release (para. 75). On the day of his release from police custody, Brau picked Mentuck up and the two travelled to a dwelling in Brandon, which was the RCMP's front house (para. 75). Mentuck was introduced to an RCMP officer who acted as both Mentuck and Brau's boss in the criminal organization. As a sign of good faith, the boss loaned the target $100.00 to buy clothes, since he had only the clothing he was wearing upon his release from custody (para. 76). Undercover operatives were able to gain the target's confidence, and Mentuck was taken in by the ruse through to the end.

Grand Prize Winner

In six cases, the targets were approached by marketing company representatives and informed that they were contest winners. In *Bridges* (2005a; featured in Chapter 1), undercover operatives went door to door in the suspect's neighbourhood posing as employees of a marketing company. Bridges was approached and asked to participate in a survey. As a result of his participation, the target was told that he and several others had won an all-expenses paid trip to a Calgary Flames National Hockey League game. Bridges attended the game with the other grand-prize winners, who were undercover police officers. During the game, one of the officers was able to befriend Bridges and, over the next few months, convince Bridges that he (the undercover officer) was a member of a criminal enterprise. Bridges was then recruited and employed by the operative on several occasions (para. 3).

In December 2000, two undercover officers approached Jean-Paul Aubee's apartment under the guise of marketers working for a legitimate beer company. He was asked to take part in a taste test and was then given instant scratch tickets. The scheme was designed to have Aubee win a free case of beer and have his scratch ticket entered into a grand prize draw, an all-expenses paid trip to a Vancouver Grizzlies NBA game (Bernhardt 2003: 5).

In a similar scenario, following a two-month program of surveillance, a female undercover operator approached Christine Lepage purporting to be a door-to-door salesperson promoting beauty products (Cherry 2005: A8). By purchasing cosmetics, Lepage was entered into a draw for a three-day trip to a spa in Montebello, Québec. She, too, was the winner of the purported contest. During this holiday "the RCMP began weaving a fake world around Ms. Lepage, slowly introducing her into what she thought was an organized crime gang" (Cherry 2005: A8).

The Use of a Third Party

In six cases, the police employed a third party (e.g., co-accused, informant, girl-friend, mother) to establish contact with the target. Two prevalent scenarios were to have an undercover operative befriend an acquaintance of the target or to use a police informer to introduce the undercover officer(s) to the target. In *Beaulac* (1997), Jacques Beaulac, the suspect's brother, became a police informer and introduced the main undercover operator to their target (White 1990: B1). The primary undercover operator approached the suspect under the pretense that he was being recruited as a drug courier for a Montreal-based gang (White 1990: B1).

In order to establish contact with Dean Christopher Roberts, an undercover police officer befriended his female companion, Ms. Ewert (*Roberts* 1997: para. 4). They enlisted her help in transporting vehicles. It was believed that this "get-rich-quick scheme" would be particularly appealing to Roberts, as "he was in straitened financial circumstances and under pressure from his creditors" (para. 5). The undercover team was successful in making a connection with Ms. Ewert, which in turn provided them with the opportunity to gain the confidence of Roberts over time.

Place of Employment/School

In five cases, RCMP operatives endeavoured to make contact with the target at their place of employment/school. Jason Dix was employed as a scale technician at Pacific Scales, where he was responsible for sales, installation, and servicing of the industrial scales (*Dix* 2002: para. 15). An undercover operative, claiming to be a member of an illicit criminal organization involved in money laundering and other illicit activities, approached Pacific Scales looking to buy a scale for his legitimate construction-development business (para. 119). The undercover officer attempted to have Dix "provide services to the operative relating to his expertise in scales 'under the table'" (para. 120). While Dix turned down this offer, he did accept the operative's proposition to help him build a deck onto his home. Dix was soon introduced to money laundering, trafficking in drugs, and various other illicit activities.

To initiate contact with Ronda Black, an undercover operative hung around Summit Career College, where Black was enrolled. The undercover's story was that she was taking a correspondence course (at another institution) and was in search of a tutor (*Black* 2007: para. 146). One day, the undercover operative initiated a scheme by purportedly locking her keys in her vehicle, then asking Black, who was fortuitously walking across the college parking lot, if she would be willing to give her a ride to pick up a spare set of keys (para. 147). Black agreed, and the two became acquaintances. Undercover officers were also successful at recruiting Paul Forknall and David Lowe at their places of employment.

Staged Breakdown of a Vehicle

In four cases, RCMP operatives were able to initiate contact with the target by staging a breakdown of their vehicle near the residence of the suspect. In *Unger* (1993a, para. 19), two undercover officers staged a breakdown just outside a farm in rural Manitoba where the twenty-year old Kyle Unger was staying. As a result, RCMP officers were able to establish a personal relationship with Unger (para. 21). In *Hathway* (2007: para. 12), the RCMP had a female undercover operative knock on Hathway's door claiming to have a flat tire. The suspect was subsequently introduced to other members of the purported criminal syndicate and engaged in its day-to-day operations. These operations included a staged beating and threats to kill a woman, her spouse, and their two-year-old child. Hathway feared for his safety and that of his child (para. 19)

Lastly, an undercover operator orchestrated a breakdown outside the dwelling of Peter William Fliss, a suspect in the first-degree murder of Jo Anne Feddema. As part of the initial relationship-building process, the undercover operator asked Fliss if he would be willing to store equipment for a marijuana grow operation and help the operative find a dwelling to rent (*Fliss* 2000: para. 46).

Other techniques that emerged from the analysis include meeting the target in a drinking establishment, and most unsettling, making contact with targets at a detoxification facility for rehabilitation of a drug and/or alcohol abuse problem. Regardless of the method chosen to initiate contact with the target, the purpose of the initial meetings is to introduce the undercover operator and the criminal syndicate to the target.

Money as a Significant Grooming Tool

In many of the scenarios, targets are involved in what appear to be a series of criminal activities. Upon completion of these purportedly illegal tasks, targets are paid small sums of cash for their efforts (small in comparison to the money they could earn once they have demonstrated themselves as loyal, honest, and trustworthy). However, to many targets, these small sums represent extraordinary payment for little effort. To convey to targets a sense of the criminal lifestyle they could potentially be leading, undercover operatives also subsidize the costs of transportation, meals, clothing, hotel accommodations, and, in some cases, cellular phones. Some scenarios might feature "business-class air travel, fancy cars, and high-end hotel rooms" (Baron 2008a: A4). Depending on the target's lifestyle choices, they might be treated to activities such as watching exotic dancers (Baron 2008a: A4).

In twenty-nine cases, there was evidence that the suspect's financial circumstances made the economic incentives offered by the criminal organization difficult to pass up. In *Evans* (1996), Mr. Justice Preston described the accused's circumstances as such:

He had barely enough money to survive at a subsistence level. The undercover operators bought him liquor, gave him money to buy drugs and shoes and bought him food. They held out to him the hope of becoming part of their organization and obtaining a secure friendship with them and their associates. They were confident, well dressed and financially comfortable. They were everything that he was not. He had no other friends. (para. 14)

Clayton George Mentuck, over the course of seven days, earned $1,800 for a series of jobs he performed for the primary undercover operator. The work was minimal in nature and took the accused roughly twenty hours to complete (*Mentuck* 2000b: para. 76). In fact, one police witness testified the remuneration "may have been more money than he'd seen in his life" (*Mentuck* 2000b: para. 99).

Wayne MacMillan's assistance to an undercover operator earned him nearly $2,000 over a three-week period (*MacMillan* 2003: para 19). During an elaborate eight-month operational plan against C.K.R.S., the accused performed over forty jobs for the organization, and was compensated over $6,700 plus expenses for his efforts (para. 37–38).[5] For one year, undercover operatives involved G.W.F. in a series of criminal activities, including delivering contraband, money laundering, and counting large sums of money received from a feigned cocaine smuggling enterprise. He was compensated a total of $5310 for his help (*G.W.F.* 2000: para. 52).

In 2002, Nelson Hart, a truck driver from Gander, Newfoundland, became the target of a Mr. Big undercover operation designed to elicit incriminating statements from him regarding his involvement in the drowning of his two daughters. Playing on the fact that he was a truck driver, members of the criminal organization offered Hart a job with DCW Trucking Company, a purportedly legitimate and lucrative cover business for the organization's criminal activity (*Hart* 2007: para. 10). Hart took on a few delivery jobs for which he was paid modest sums of money. Once the police succeeded in establishing a level of rapport with Hart, they introduced him to the criminal enterprise aspect of the organization, including dealing in fake credit cards, forged passports, and fake casino chips (para. 17). As the scenarios progressed, Hart was given increased responsibilities and remuneration for his help. He travelled from St. John's to Halifax to Montreal and Vancouver at the organization's expense, staying in some of Canada's finest hotels and dining at some of its most opulent restaurants (para. 23). In total, Hart earned $15,720 for his participation in various purported activities (Brautigam 2007b: A8).

Financial inducements do not stop here. The relatively innocuous jobs that targets perform up to this point are nothing compared to the "big deal" or the promise of membership in the powerful and wealthy criminal organization. If the target can prove his or her loyalty to the organization by disclosing details of a criminal past, he or she will be permitted to assist in a major criminal undertaking, earn thousands of dollars, and potentially secure a permanent position in the syndicate.

By setting up a legitimate business for the criminal organization and allowing its members to use this business as a method to launder money, Jason Dix could, he was told, earn up to $100,000 a year (*Dix* 2002: para. 133). In *Bonisteel* (2008), the accused accompanied an undercover operative to a bank, where they deposited $80,000 into a safe deposit box. The operative told the target that the key to the box and the $80,000 would be his once the job, a large drug shipment to be offloaded on Vancouver Island, was done (para. 16). In the same way, O.N.E. was promised a key to a safety deposit box containing $U.S. 50,000 (*O.N.E.* 2000a: para. 25). What's more, upon completion of the drug offload, O.N.E. was told the organization would send her vacationing in Mexico, where she would stay until the "heat" subsided (para. 26).

In *Mentuck* (2000b), the authorities employed the "fall guy" scenario. Undercover operatives explained to Mentuck that once the fall guy was convicted of the murder, the organization would provide him with a lawyer and the necessary financing to file a civil suit against the government for being wrongfully charged with and jailed for the murder (para. 90). Mr. Big told Mentuck that his lawyer estimated the settlement to be one million dollars and that Mentuck would stand to gain substantial proceeds from the lawsuit, a minimum of $85,000 or 10 percent of the settlement, whichever was the greater (*Mentuck* 2000b: para. 90). Also, the accused would be granted an ongoing position with the criminal organization (*Mentuck* 2000b: para. 99).

Such inducements are likely to produce exaggerated or false statements. As defence lawyer Daniel Brodsky explained, "You know that old cliche, everybody has a price? You can get anybody to confess, as long as you have enough time and the person understands when they're confessing that there's no consequence" (Brautigam 2007c: A4).

Eliciting a Confession

The courts have sanctioned the use of deceptive police methods in a non-custodial context, and law enforcement agencies have effectively pushed the boundaries of acceptable interrogation practices. That is to say, the use of subterfuge, holding out strong inducements, and veiled threats of violence is tolerated in the investigation of particularly serious crimes so long as the tactics are not offensive to the integrity of the judicial process (*McIntyre* 1994; *Roberts* 1997; *Rothman* 1981; *Unger* 1993a). Figure 2 shows seven distinct methods used to obtain confessions in the Mr. Big scenarios in this study: 1) the use of corrupt police contacts; 2) the introduction of a "fall guy"; 3) the production of false documentation; 4) the claim of authority to destroy physical evidence; 5) an offer to fabricate an alibi; 6) an offer to enlist the help of an "expert" to help the target defeat lie-detector test; and 7) an offer to frame someone else.

Figure 2: Techniques Used to Procure a Confession

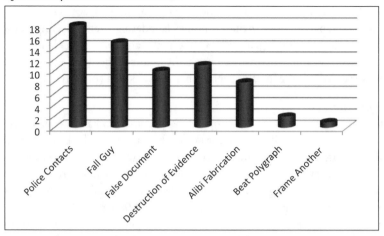

Corrupt Police Contacts on the Organization's Payroll

Employed in eighteen cases, this ruse involves the boss and/or his associates suggesting that they, as criminals, have contacts within police departments who grant them access to sensitive police information, which helps undercover operatives check the veracity of their targets' admissions. Targets are also informed that the inside contacts can, for example, destroy incriminating evidence to help steer the murder investigation away from the targets. In *Redd* (1999), the undercover RCMP operative posing as the main contact for the criminal organization informed the target that the organization had contacts that permeated all levels of the criminal justice system, "including police, judges, even personnel in the prosecutor's office" (para. 160). As part of the grooming process, the undercover operatives involved Redd in various simulated crimes, including debt collection by use of threats, transportation of weapons, and drug deliveries. He was also asked to take a contract with the organization to kill a woman (para. 158).

In *Grandinetti* (2005), undercover officers employed a standard Mr. Big scenario, posing as an "international organization involved in drug trafficking and money laundering" (para. 7). The criminal enterprise attempted to gain Grandinetti's confidence but was unsuccessful. After several failed attempts to get the accused to talk about his aunt's murder, investigators tried to convince Grandinetti "that they had contacts in the police department who were prepared to act unlawfully, and that they had been able to use those contacts in the past to influence an investigation" (para. 9). To demonstrate this ability, undercover officers used their corrupt police contacts to find out the name of the lead investigator on the Grandinetti murder case. Operatives then suggested that the organization could steer the murder investigation away from the target, but that he was a liability to their organization because of the ongoing investigations. They communicated to him that he would lose out on a profitable career as the organization's "Calgary contact." In order to gain his trust, the undercover operatives engaged Grandinetti "in various criminal activities, including money laundering, theft, receiving illegal firearms and drug dealing" (para. 10). Grandinetti subsequently made inculpatory statements regarding his involvement in the murder of his aunt, and then led undercover officers to the location where his aunt was killed (para. 10).

The Fall Guy

In fifteen of eighty-one cases, RCMP operatives proposed to have a confederate suffering from a terminal illness take the fall for the crime(s) under investigation, provided the target supply Mr. Big with enough details to make the confession believable. The target was told that even the smallest mundane details were absolutely necessary because the fall guy would likely undergo a series of police interviews before his admission of guilt was accepted (*Mentuck* 2000b: para. 90).

In order to secure the murder weapon from suspect Michael Caster, RCMP operatives suggested a "Henry fall guy" plot (*Caster* 1998: para. 8). Henry was a terminally ill employee of the criminal syndicate who was prepared to take the blame for the murder in question so long as the organization would take care of his family financially. The intent was to have Caster produce the murder weapon so that Henry could put his fingerprints on the gun, subsequently linking him to the murder. In addition, the crime boss offered to provide Caster with an alibi for the time of the murder (*Caster* 1998: para. 9). The undercover officers also discussed with Caster the possibility of a contract killing of someone who was skimming money from the organization (para. 6). Caster, wary that his friends might be undercover police officers, was reluctant to go along with the proposed Henry scenario. To help him develop more comfort with and trust in the organization, operatives engaged Caster in a major criminal undertaking, a purported off-loading of hashish (paras. 10–11).

Producing a Fictitious Internal Police Memorandum

In ten instances, Mr. Big showed the target during a purported organizational meeting a police memorandum indicating that he or she was suspected of involvement in the crime under investigation. For example, after several failed attempts to elicit a confession from Sebastian Burns and Atif Rafay concerning their roles in the Bellevue murders of Rafay's family, Mr. Big advised the accused that police had secured vital DNA evidence from the crime scene that implicated them in the murders. At a meeting between Burns and Mr. Big, the boss revealed a fabricated police document purporting to establish his involvement in the murder of the Rafay family. The document, written on official Bellevue Police Department letterhead, claimed that hair found at the murder scene incriminated Burns in the murders. This ruse was also designed to impress upon Burns and Rafay that undercover operatives had connections with corrupt Bellevue officers (Jiwa 2004: A24). Mr. Big then suggested he would "set fire to the records room of the Bellevue police department, switch Burns' hair samples at the crime lab, and get an East Indian to confess to the murder" (Ogilvie 1996: A5). Following his appraisal of the document, Burns disclosed his and Rafay's role in the murders (*United States of America v. Burns* 1997: para. 4). The following day, Rafay was brought into the hotel room where Burns not only showed him the report but also informed Rafay that he disclosed everything to Mr. Big. It was then suggested that Rafay explain his role in the homicides because Mr. Big "needed to trust Rafay not to inform on Burns" (para. 4). When Rafay admitted to killing his family for money, Mr. Big said, "Hey, don't be embarrassed. Everything I do is for money. I don't give two f—s what you did to your family" (Baron 2008a: A4).

In *Forknall* (2000), under the guise of a criminal organization intending to receive a large shipment of drugs, police offered both targets an opportunity to earn $20,000–$30,000 for helping to offload the shipment, so long as they were found to be suitable to join the organization (para. 7). During a purported organizational meeting, the crime boss and his assistant showed one of the targets fabricated documents that had the appearance of being extracted from the Police Information Retrieval System (PIRS) and contained information establishing Copeland and Forknall's involvement in the first-degree murder of Tiffany McKinney (*Forknall* 2000: para. 9). Copeland and Forknall continued to tell different stories about the disappearance of the victim. Police then initiated a meeting between the co-accused, Mr. Big, and an undercover police officer posing as someone within the organization that had expertise in disposing of bodies and covering traces of crime (para. 12). This tactic, combined with a reminder of the importance of honesty and trustworthiness, persuaded both men to tell police independently that they had planned to kill McKinney for her car and dispose of the body (para. 12). Copeland and Forknall also independently led police to the burial site, where police were able to recover the body (para. 6).

Destruction of Evidence

As indicated in Figure 2, this stratagem proved to be effective in eleven cases. Operatives quite simply proposed to divert charges by either disposing of or destroying evidence. As mentioned in Chapter 1, Michael Bridges became a target of an undercover operation designed to investigate the disappearance of his ex-girlfriend (*Bridges* 2005: para. 16). Bridges would come to understand that Mr. Big, through his extensive connections, had been made aware of a "problem" in Bridges' past, namely that he was the primary suspect in the murder of his ex-girlfriend. Bridges was told that the criminal organization could retrieve the body and dispose of the evidence (para. 19). Upon verification of the details by his sources, Mr. Big vowed to make "the problem" go away and secure Bridges' future role in the organization.

Alibi Fabrication

When the target is "unable" to account for his or her whereabouts during the material time(s), undercover operatives suggest that the organization might be able to assist in fabricating an alibi to account for the discrepancy, provided the target's story checks out. As shown in Figure 2, the alibi fabrication ruse was employed in eight cases. In *Bicknell* (2003), an undercover police officer posing as the main contact for the criminal organization suggested that he could assist the accused by arranging for him to be seen on video at a local casino. The undercover officer would then retrieve the tape and alter the date and times to account for Bicknell's whereabouts during the time in question (para. 101).

In order to get Jason Joseph "on board" as part of the purported criminal organization, Mr. Big and one of his criminal counterparts suggested a scheme in which an alibi would be created by having the suspect use false credit cards at a Montreal hotel bar (*Joseph* 2000a: paras. 44–45). Later, counsel for the accused argued that the alibi scheme concocted by undercover operatives (i.e., fabrication of evidence) was an obstruction of justice. However, Mr. Justice Taylor concluded that the undercover officers never intended to provide Joseph with an alibi or to engage in a conspiracy to obstruct justice: "To do so would defeat the very object of the exercise: to obtain evidence of admissions upon which to prosecute the two accused for the offence of attempted murder" (para. 75). The holding out of the possibility that an alibi would be provided was contingent on the accused providing officers with information about the crime so that the alibi could be created (para. 73).

We Can Help You Beat It

While a polygraph examination is not admissible as evidence in court to show whether an accused is lying or telling the truth, law enforcement agencies use it with increasing frequency as an investigative tool (*Oickle* 2000: para. 88). As such, Mr. Big's suggestion to targets that he will hire an "expert" to help the target beat a polygraph examination holds some weight with the target. This scheme, exemplified in *Fischer* (2005), was employed in two cases.

On the evening of May 15, 1999, the police were called to Lily Lake Road, thirteen kilometres outside of Merritt, British Columbia, after a group of horseback riders from the lower mainland discovered the body of sixteen-year-old Darci Drefko. Patrick Fischer quickly came under suspicion, as he was the last person seen in the company of the deceased (*Fischer* 2005: para. 3). He would soon become the target of a Mr. Big scenario. In a meeting with Mr. Big at the Sheraton Hotel in Guildford at Surrey, the boss stressed that he was not willing to take risks with people he did not know. He then produced a fictitious police report which implicated Fischer in Drefko's death (para. 14). The boss gave Fischer two options to make the investigation disappear: a DNA test or a polygraph test. Although Fischer was eager to secure a $20,000 payoff from a feigned drug deal, he was reluctant to participate in any tests, fearing investigators would sabotage or manipulate the tests to implicate him in the murder (para. 34). Fischer and members of the local RCMP detachment had an abysmal relationship (paras. 5, 32).

Fischer indicated that he would be prepared to take the test but only if Mr. Big could guarantee that he would pass, because he did not trust the police (para. 14). This led to considerable discussion about the possibility of the boss's enlisting the help of an "expert" to help the accused defeat the lie detector test, which in turn, led to Fischer disclosing details about the murder:

> Okay here's what's what's going to happen, I'm going to get my guy, I'm going to get him up here, he comes out of the states, we'll get a hotel room and he's going to sit down and he's going to teach you how beat that fucking polygraph. It's simple, you're right, you are, you are 100 percent right when you say, it can be fucking beat, you're a smart guy that way. Okay, but he's going to want some background, so what Pat says in this room, stays in this room, okay, we don't have to tell Bert, I'm not going to tell Bert, and I'd prefer you just keep your mouth shut. (para. 14)

According to the investigators, they did not disclose the location of the body or the cause of death. Although Fischer maintained he was able to piece together details of the crime from what others told him, in his confession to undercover police officers he disclosed information related to the cause of death and led the police to a site that was less than one hundred yards from where the body was found (*Fischer* 2005: para. 20). Linda Fischer, Patrick's mother, maintains that the holdback evidence was compromised and that her son's confession was contaminated by numerous sources.[6]

Framing Someone Else

This scheme has undercover operatives suggesting that they can change the course of the investigation against the target by framing someone else. David Wytyshyn was the primary suspect in the murder investigation of his landlady's death. Knowing that Wytyshyn was the subject of this police investigation, an undercover officer who purportedly belonged to a criminal organization recruiting Wytyshyn offered to help frame another tenant for his landlady's murder (*Wytyshyn* 2002: para. 4). In order to have this done, however, Wytyshyn would have to disclose as much as possible about his involvement in the murder so as "to give credibility to the setup by ensuring that the information disclosed matched what had been discovered through police investigation" (para. 4).

As evidenced in the preceding section, undercover police officers employ a range of tactics to offset the inherent difficulties of eliciting self-incriminating statements from targets. It is important to note that these methods are not mutually exclusive; undercover operatives may employ a combination of strategies to extract a confession from targets. In addition to the use of money to groom their targets, undercover police officers also use feigned assaults and other criminal activities to bond with their targets.

Notes

1. There were three co-accused in one case and two co-accused in 10 of the eighty-one cases.
2. Information on age was available for eighty-eight out of the ninety-three accused.
3. See Mr. Justice Williams' analysis in *Perovic* (2004b) at paras. 25–27, which will be discussed in greater detail below. See also Waye (2003).
4. As discussed above, sixteen of the ninety-three accused pleaded guilty and are not included in this table.
5. Since each scenario required a significant amount of travel, officers financed his trips, paying for accommodations, air travel, or transportation by bus. In addition, he was given two cellular phones so that he could remain in contact with gang members (para. 37).
6. For more on this case see <http://www.injusticebusters.com/06/Fischer,%20Patrick. shtml>.

4

Mr. Big: Legal, Moral, and Ethical Issues

An analysis of the eighty-one decisions revealed several recurring legal issues raised by the Mr. Big undercover tactic. This chapter examines the following: 1) the question of whether the target has a right to silence protected by the common law and section 7 of the *Canadian Charter of Rights and Freedoms*; 2) the applicability of the law on voluntariness of confessions and its persons-in-authority requirement; 3) the issue of whether the Mr. Big technique is tantamount to an abuse of process; 4) the question of whether an admission from the accused is an exception to the hearsay rule requiring the establishment of necessity and reliability; 5) the judicial and academic concern with false confessions; 6) the admissibility of narrative evidence that tends to show bad character or a criminal disposition; and 7) the rewriting of criminal law to accommodate Mr. Big investigations. The chapter closes with some comments about the moral and ethical issues surrounding Mr. Big operations.

Right to Silence as Protected by the Common Law and Section 7 of the Canadian Charter of Rights and Freedoms

Everyone has a right to remain silent in the face of questioning from state authorities. This is made clear by Mme. Justice Abella in *Turcotte*:

> The common law right to silence exists at all times against the state, whether or not the person asserting it is within its power or control. Like the confessions rule, an accused's right to silence applies any time he or she interacts with a person in authority, whether detained or not. It is a right premised on an individual's freedom to choose the extent of his or her cooperation with the police, and is animated by a recognition of the potentially coercive impact of the state's authority and a concern that individuals not be required to incriminate themselves. These policy considerations exist both before and after arrest or detention. There is, as a result, no principled basis for failing to extend the common law right to silence to both periods. (2005, para. 51)

What is unclear is why the right to remain silent disappears when police officers masquerade as criminals enticing suspects into a world of crime (some real, some fake) in order to get the suspects to brag about offences (usually murders) they may, or may not, have committed. The hollowness of the right to silence is most obvious when the police target suspects after they refuse to talk to the police, either in or out of custody. Many of the Mr. Big investigations in this study involved suspects who, prior to being targeted by a Mr. Big investigation, refused to talk to or assist the police. Indeed, their refusal to cooperate was often a prerequisite to a Mr. Big investigation. If the undercover operatives had been identified as police officers, none of these interrogation-induced confessions would be admissible. The case for suspects' right to remain silent becomes even stronger when detained suspects who refuse to speak to authorities are released so that they can be targeted by a Mr. Big operation (see argument by Palmer 2004).

The Supreme Court of Canada seems to have exported the confession rule's prerequisite of a "person in authority" to the common law right to remain silent. This is clear in the above quotation from Mme. Justice Abella in *Turcotte*. She also appears to accept the "coercive power of the state" as a prerequisite to citizens' right to remain silent. In an earlier decision, Mme. Justice McLachlin delineated the right to remain silent under section 7 of the *Charter*, suggesting that this right exists only when a person is in detention or control by the state:

> The jurisprudence relating to the right to silence has never extended protection against police tricks to the pre-detention period. Nor does the *Charter* extend the right to counsel to pre-detention investigations. The two circumstances are quite different. In an undercover operation prior to detention, the individual from whom information is sought is not in the control of the state. There is no need to protect him from the greater power of the state. After detention, the situation is quite different, the state takes control and assumes the responsibility of ensuring that the detainee's rights are respected. (*Hebert* 1990: para. 74)

Mr. Big undercover operations are conducted during the investigatory phase; targets are considered suspects but are not in detention at the material time they make statements to undercover police. The Clifford Moore case offers an illustration. Moore was suspected of being criminally involved in the death of Vaughn Davis, whose body was located just outside Valemount, B.C. (*Moore* 1997: para. 1). Police suspicions intensified when investigating officers discovered Moore's palm prints at the crime scene. The decision to mount an undercover operation against him was made (para. 5). The elaborate crime boss ruse culminated in a meeting between the target and several undercover police officers (para. 6). The target voluntarily accompanied undercover operatives to Jasper Park Lodge, was checked into a hotel room and given a hundred dollars in cash (para. 17). The defence claimed that these circumstances were "tantamount to a detention" because of the degree of control undercover police officers exerted over Moore (para. 15). In particular, counsel claimed that Moore "had no means of transportation independent of the undercover police" who transported him to Jasper, Alberta (para. 15). In rejecting the argument of Moore's counsel, Mme. Justice Proudfoot concluded that the atmosphere created by the undercover operation did not amount to detention because the appellant accompanied undercover officers to Jasper voluntarily. Furthermore, he could have used the hundred dollars to purchase a bus ticket home. Since Moore was not detained, the undercover officers could not have breached his right to remain silent under section 7 of the *Charter* (para. 19).

The New Brunswick Court of Appeal examined another Mr. Big operation (*McIntyre* 1993), to determine if McIntyre's statements to an undercover police officer after he was arrested and released for lack of evidence unfairly deprived him of his constitutional right to silence (para. 47). The RCMP initiated a Mr. Big ruse by first placing a "cell plant," an undercover officer posing as a criminal, in McIntyre's cell. The "plant" was introduced to McIntyre as a "Montreal criminal involved in the illegal cigarette trade, prostitution and other criminal activities" (para. 35). Once this contact was made, McIntyre was released for want of evidence (para. 47). Having shared the cell, however, the undercover officer had learned vital information about where the suspect lived and could arrange to run into McIntyre once he was released. Having gained the target's trust, undercover operatives offered him a job with the organization contingent on his ability to kill. McIntyre subsequently made inculpatory statements about his involvement in the alleged murder (para. 37).

Mr. Justice Rice, dissenting in the New Brunswick Court of Appeal decision, found that the "cell plant" operation undertaken by police had its "beginnings during detention," and "successfully continued afterward" (para. 15). Citing Mme. Justice McLachlin in *Hebert* (1990), he concluded that the police subterfuge was compelling enough to undermine the appellant's constitutional right not to speak to the authorities (para. 17). By admitting into evidence a statement obtained in this manner — that is conscripted — Rice said, "the Court could give the impression that it excuses or tolerates such deliberate conduct, the purpose of which is to exceed constitutional limits, or even that it condones such an attitude" (para. 21). Writing the majority decision, however, Mr. Justice Ayles found that the appellant was not being detained for investigative purposes. Rather, "he was detained for a few hours and then released" (para. 54). What's more, there was no reason to protect McIntyre from the power of the state because he chose to become involved with the criminal organization, was free to come and go, and could have withdrawn from the organization at any time (para. 55). Thus, according to the majority, the actions taken by police did not violate the principles of fundamental justice. This ground of appeal was subsequently dismissed (para. 56). On further appeal to the Supreme Court of Canada, Mr. Justice Gonthier, for the Court, agreed with the majority of the New Brunswick Court of Appeal, finding that the appellant "was not detained within the meaning of *Hebert and Broyles*," and also observed that the police trickery employed would not be so offensive as to shock the community (para. 1). The one-paragraph oral judgment was delivered without any detailed analysis; however, such an analysis may be warranted in the future.

We argue that the right to remain silent ought to extend to pre-detention deception of this sort.[1] The extent of grooming (discussed in Chapter 3) and the irresistible inducements in Mr. Big scenarios put the undercover officers in control of their targets. In some cases, otherwise law-abiding individuals are socialized into a life of crime and degradation. This type of mental control can be much more powerful in inducing false confessions than confining a suspect behind bars. The right to silence becomes meaningless if the police can simply switch to undercover operations to by-pass the right to remain silent and trick a suspect to talk to them.

The Confessions Rule: The Law on Voluntariness and the Person in Authority Requirement

As stated earlier, the confessions rule ensures that out-of-court statements made by an accused to a person in authority are admissible as evidence only if the statements are voluntary (*Hodgson* 1998; *Oickle* 2000). In twenty-seven cases, defence counsel submitted that the accused's self-incriminating statements to undercover police officers should have been excluded since the admissions were a product of implied threats, psychological manipulation, and/or significant inducements held out by persons in authority. In all but one case (*Roop* 2007),[2] the courts consistently ruled that from both a subjective and an objectively reasonable standard, the accused perceived the undercover officers to be criminal cohorts, and were unaware of the undercover officers' true identity. For example, Justice Marc Rosenberg, for the Ontario Court of Appeal in *Osmar* (2007a), stated, "Although the statements are invariably induced by promises made by persons in authority," the issue of voluntariness, at common law, does not arise because the suspect is not aware of the true identity of undercover officers (para. 3).

The effect of the Supreme Court of Canada's decision in *Grandinetti* (2005) is that undercover police officers who claim to be able to influence the course of an investigation through their corrupt police contacts are not persons in authority; thus a confession coerced by such officers falls outside the ambit of the confessions rule. RCMP operatives shared a story with Grandinetti about what they were able to do for "Dan," a member of the organization implicated in a murder; by using his connections to make a witness disappear and to retrieve vital, incriminating evidence, the boss of the criminal syndicate managed to have the murder charges reduced to aggravated assault (*Grandinetti* 2005: para. 9). Undercover police officers had claimed that they could use their corrupt police contacts to protect Grandinetti from further police investigation. At trial, the defence argued that the boss and his criminal associates were, in effect, persons in authority because they proposed to enlist the help of corrupt police officers to influence the investigation against Grandinetti (para. 13). Mme. Justice Abella, writing on behalf of the court, held that "the state's coercive power is not engaged" when a suspect confesses to undercover police officers who claim to enlist the help of corrupt criminal justice officials to thwart the interests of the state (para. 44). In the end, the issue for the jury is whether the statement made by the accused is reliable and true (see *Carter* 2001: para. 64).

Speaking for the majority in *Hodgson* (1998), Mr. Justice Cory remarked that the common law confessions rule is calibrated to deter the use of improper coercive tactics by the state (para. 29). Although he acknowledged that a statement to a person not in authority could sometimes be made in such coercive circumstances that the reliability of the admission would be jeopardized (para. 26), he declined to eliminate the person in authority requirement, and urged Parliament to address the issue. Mr. Justice Cory added,

> In the meantime I would suggest that in circumstances where a statement of the accused is obtained by a person who is not a person in authority by means of degrading treatment such as violence or threats of violence, a clear direction should be given to the jury as to the dangers of relying upon it. The direction might include words such as these: "A statement obtained as a result of inhuman or degrading treatment or the use of violence or threats of violence may not be the manifestation of the exercise of a free will to confess. Rather, it may result solely from the oppressive treatment or fear of such treatment. If it does, the statement may very well be either unreliable or untrue. Therefore if you conclude that the statement was obtained by such oppression very little if any weight should be attached to it." (para. 30)

This has become known as the "Hodgson warning." As Mme. Justice Ryan observed in *Carter* (2001), the purpose of this warning "is to bring home to a jury that a confession obtained under oppressive or fearful circumstances may not be reliable and must be scrutinized with care. Self-preservation is a natural human instinct that may lead a person to confess to something he or she did not do simply to bring an end to the misery of the situation" (para. 59). She did, however, find that the warning was not necessary in the circumstances of *Carter*'s trial (para. 60), which took place after the *Hodgson* decision (para. 58).

Does the Mr. Big Operation Amount to an Abuse of Process?

At what point do the tactics employed by police during the undercover operation become egregious enough to shock the conscience of the community? In *Rothman* (1981), Mr. Justice Lamer noted that the courts should be vigilant not to unduly limit police discretion:

> It must also be borne in mind that the investigation of crime and the detection of criminals is not a game to be governed by the Marquess of Queensbury rules. The authorities, in dealing with shrewd and often sophisticated criminals, must sometimes of necessity resort to tricks or other forms of deceit and should not through the rule be hampered in their work. What should be repressed vigorously is conduct on their part that shocks the community (697)[3]

In seventeen of the eighty-one cases, the defence challenged the admissibility of self-incriminating statements obtained during the undercover sting operation, arguing that the tactics "transgressed the bounds of acceptable" police conduct (*Terrico* 2005: para. 3). The verisimilitude of such undercover operations, as described in the Introduction, is impressive. To convince the target that undercover officers are hardened and ruthless criminals, RCMP operatives utilize a range of tactics, including violence, intimidation, psychological manipulation, and implied threats of physical harm (i.e., feigned assaults/murders, threats of death or serious bodily harm).

In *Unger* (1993a), counsel for the accused submitted that the Mr. Big operation was "unfair in its implementation and design" and amounted to an abuse of process, which violated Unger's section 7 rights under the *Charter* (para. 55). Since Unger's confession stemmed from the "grand inducement" of membership in a criminal organization, counsel argued that his statements should have been excluded from evidence (para. 56). The Manitoba Court of Appeal, however, affirmed the Manitoba Court of Queen's Bench decision that the evidence in question was admissible and that the tactics employed by undercover operatives would not shock the conscience of the community. Chief Justice Scott went on to say that "Courts should not be setting public policy on the parameters of undercover operations" (para. 69). Moreover, it was the Court's view that, in light of the heinous circumstances surrounding the death of sixteen-year-old Brigitte Grenier, and given the lack of evidence, the public would endorse rather than be shocked by the efforts of the undercover police officers. The Manitoba Court of Appeal also held that undercover operatives did not subvert Unger's right to remain silent, guaranteed by section 7 of the *Charter*, because he was not detained or under arrest at the material time. The Court was of the view that Unger "was not coerced against his will or tricked into making a confession" (para. 78). We return to the Unger case in our Chapter 5 discussion of wrongful convictions.

The relation of fear to coercion is complicated in such operations. In *United States of America v. Burns* (1997), an undercover operator testified that criminal organizations are "held together with violence and that the trust that is often associated with criminal organizations is based on a fear of reprisal for anyone who betrays the criminal organization" (para. 4). He told the accused that betraying the organization or a member thereof could lead to extreme violence against that person or that person's family (para. 4). To illustrate his point, the undercover officer referred to an incident where Mr. Big arranged to have someone disposed of because he informed on the organization.

Justice Romilly opined in *Riley* (2001) that "Instilling fear in the accused is not necessarily coercion resulting in an abuse of process" (para. 24). Notwithstanding the fearful atmosphere that resonates throughout the undercover investigation, the director of undercover operations in British Columbia, Staff Sgt. Peter Marsh, stated that undercover operatives do not normally issue direct threats to targets; instead, such threats are merely implied (Hutchinson 2004: RB1). A lawyer representing the RCMP asks, "Why would we want to create that kind of fear... Why would we want to put that on the table for a trier of fact to diminish our case" (Baron 2008a:

70

A4). Furthermore, as Mr. Justice Iacobucci observed in *Oickle* (2000) (although speaking about a confession to a person in authority), "any confession that is the product of outright violence is involuntary and unreliable" (para. 53).

To convince David Lowe that the criminal organization he was dealing with had a known capacity for violence, officers staged a hostage-taking scenario. The female hostage was depicted as the girlfriend of a former gang member who owed Jason, the main undercover operator, a sum of money. Armed with a handgun, Jason acted violently toward the hostage and threatened to kill her and her boyfriend (*Lowe* 2004: para. 249). On numerous occasions, other undercover operatives posing as Jason's associates would act frightened or highly respectful of him (para. 232). In a comparable scenario, Wilfred Hathway witnessed a feigned assault upon a woman who was covered in blood and then forcibly thrown into the trunk of a car. One of the undercover operatives threatened to kill her, her spouse, and their two-year-old child (*Hathway* 2007: para. 19).

During a feigned drug deal in *O.N.E.* (2000a), the accused witnessed an undercover operative become enraged with someone he suspected of being a "rat" (para. 33). Consequently, uc1, posing as the main contact for the criminal organization, sent another operative to retrieve a "piece and muffler" (gun and silencer) (para. 34). O.N.E. was made to overhear this conversation. She also witnessed the purportedly vicious beating of the individual who informed on the organization (para. 35). uc1 testified that the scenario was intended to show the suspect that the criminal organization did not take kindly to persons who betrayed the organization, and that its members would unhesitatingly resort to deadly force (para. 37).

In *Roberts* (1997), the defence position at trial and on appeal was that the Mr. Big investigation amounted to an abuse of process and a violation of the accused's section 7 *Charter* rights. Writing for the Court, Mr. Justice Hall rejected Roberts' submission, stating that a reasonable, well-informed member of the community would "unhesitatingly endorse" the tactics (para. 15). Mr. Justice Hall chose the trenchant words of Mr. Justice Scollin of the Manitoba Queen's Bench, in *Skinner* (1992), to express what he thought could be fairly said about the appellant as well as the police undercover activities:

> The difference between the unpalatable and the inedible is generally a matter of personal taste. Absent "dirty tricks," the courts should not set themselves up as the arbiters of good taste or of the preferred methods of investigation. It is unrealistic to demand chivalry from those who must investigate what are often heinous offences against blameless victims. The law should not appear to materialize as a revolutionary rabbit from a judicial magician's hat. Both the common law and the *Charter* justly preserve the accused from coercion and endow him with specific rights which he may exercise at the time of his arrest and while he is in custody; but the courts should not be so indulgent as

to preserve the accused from himself and his own untrammeled tongue, and should require realistic justification for suppressing facts from the jury which go to weight rather than to admissibility. (para. 14)

Operation Kabaya, a thirteen-month ruse aimed at procuring a confession from Jason Dix, is unquestionably one that not only embraces the spirit of violence but also pushes the envelope of how far police were willing to go. In a scenario referred to as "Whack at Yaak," the RCMP staged an elaborate drug deal gone horribly wrong. Dix and an undercover operative drove to a rural area outside of Yaak, British Columbia. Dix would remain in the vehicle as a lookout while the operative went into the dwelling to make the exchange (*Dix* 2002: para. 126). Suddenly, Dix heard gunshots and saw the operative emerge wielding a sawed-off shotgun. The operative then faced the dwelling, fired two shots inside, and ran to the vehicle. He got rid of the firearm in the woods, got into the vehicle, and explained to Dix that the victim had tried to cheat him out of money and drugs (para. 127).

Dix was left with the impression that if he divulged this information to police he would be killed, and that several statements made by undercover operatives constituted clear threats (para. 130). Despite extreme pressure applied by undercover operatives, Dix vehemently denied any involvement in the two murders under investigation (para. 131). In 2002, he was awarded $765,000 in damages in a lawsuit against the Attorney General of Canada and others. Mr. Justice Ritter ruled that the "the police clearly did significantly and seriously cross that line," and that the undercover operation was so invasive that it breached his right to privacy under sections 7 and 8 of the *Charter* (*Dix* 2002: para. 547).

The case of Wesley Evans demonstrates how over-zealousness policing and poor training, in combination with psychological attributes of the target, such as diminished cognitive functioning, put some individuals at increased risk to give false self-incriminating statements when subjected to the pressures of modern psychological interrogation techniques. This case is a "perfect storm" of sorts, in which a combination of adverse factors led to the accused providing undercover operatives with unreliable, misleading, and erroneous statements. It also led to scenarios where the undercover operatives discussed the possibility of the organization killing two people for Evans (1996: paras. 17–22).

Dr. Pos, a psychiatrist, and witness for the defence, testified at Evans' first trial that the accused had an I.Q. "roughly of between 70 and 80" and that he was "intellectually and emotionally immature and had a mental age of approximately 14" (*Evans* 1988: para. 7). He also stated that Evans was "passive-aggressive and would be susceptible to suggestion by any questioner" (para. 7). At the Supreme Court of Canada, Mme. Justice McLachlin found him to be an individual "of subnormal mental capacity" (*Evans* 1991: para. 6). At Evans' second trial, Dr. Robert Ley, a clinical psychologist, testified that he was highly suggestible and would do or say anything in order to be accepted by his newfound friends (*Evans* 1996:

para. 24). Dr. Noone, a forensic psychiatrist, testified that Evans "sometimes used words calculated to impress without understanding them. His verbal ability was such that it was easy to overestimate his intelligence" (para. 23). His personality development had been affected by a head injury sustained as a child and "by the traumatic effect of his prolonged hospitalizations" following third-degree burns incurred at the age of eleven (para. 23).

In 1988, at the age of twenty-one, Wesley Evans was tried and convicted of the 1984 and 1985 murders of two British Columbia women. Initially, authorities believed that Evans' brother, Ronald, was responsible for the murders, while a police wiretap led investigators to suspect that Wesley Evans was trafficking in marijuana (*Evans* 1988: para. 3). Detectives formed a plan to arrest Wesley on a charge of trafficking in marijuana "in the hope that he would say something to implicate his brother in the murders" (para. 19). At the time of Wesley's arrest, investigators were informed of his diminished cognitive functioning and were told to ensure he was informed of his rights. When asked if he understood his constitutional rights, Evans replied, "no." Yet the two arresting officers tried no further to explain his *Charter* rights (*Evans* 1991: para. 13).

Following a series of three interviews in which investigators claimed to have found his fingerprints at one of the crime scenes, evidence that was false, Wesley Evans confessed to the murders. Significantly, the focus of the prosecution's case was the confession evidence gathered over the course of the interviews, and a written statement from the accused, in which he confessed to both murders (*Evans* 1988: para. 47). Dr. Pos testified that Evans' confession was unreliable because his "answers followed a series of suggestive questions with Evans trying to please the investigators" (*Evans* 1988: para. 60). Indeed, research has shown that persons with intellectual deficits have a desire to please and are easily intimidated by persons in a position of authority (Drizin and Leo 2004; Everington and Fullero 1999; Gudjonsson 2003b).

At trial, Mr. Justice Callaghan rejected defence counsel's arguments that Evan's confession was obtained in violation of sections 10(a) and (b) of the *Charter*, and should have been excluded in accordance with s. 24(2) of the *Charter*. He found that the investigators had acted in good faith (*Evans* 1991: paras. 24–25). A jury convicted Evans of two counts of first-degree murder.

Evans appealed to the British Columbia Court of Appeal, but to no avail. Mme. Justice Southin, for the principal judgment, stated that even if there was a breach of Evans' *Charter* rights, "nothing could bring the administration of justice into greater disrepute than freeing a confessed murderer to kill again" (1991: para. 26). On further appeal to the Supreme Court of Canada, Madame Justice McLachlin concluded not only that Evans' admissions were "highly unreliable," but that "significant portions of the evidence which undermines the reliability of the statements was not before the jury" (para. 60). She concluded that the statements made by the appellant "should never have been admitted" into evidence and that, since they were obtained in violation of Evans' *Charter* rights, their admission would have brought the administration of justice into disrepute (*Evans* 1991: para. 65). After Wesley Evans had served approximately five years of his sentence, the Supreme Court of Canada set aside his conviction and entered an acquittal.

After his release from prison, the RCMP set up a three-month program of surveillance on Evans, following a series of complaints about "bizarre behaviour on his part" (*Evans* 1996: para. 4). Having failed to obtain sufficient incriminating evidence against him, the RCMP decided to conduct a Mr. Big sting. Mr. Justice Preston observed that the operation was conducted "on the premise that Mr. Evans was guilty of the 1984–85 murders and that his acquittal 'had something to do with the *Charter*.' None of the police officers involved read the reasons for judgment of the Supreme Court of Canada" (*Evans* 1996: para. 4). Early on in the investigation, officers had asked a psychologist for advice about how to conduct the undercover operation. They were advised "not make suggestions of a criminal nature to Evans because he 'would do anything to impress them'" (para. 9).

Officers intentionally disregarded the psychologist's advice, involving their target in a series of increasingly serious criminal exploits (para. 13). As Mr. Justice Preston pointed out, "The climate created by the undercover operators was a climate of lawlessness and killing in which they did what they wanted to their great financial profit and were protected by the resources of the 'organization'" (para. 13). When operatives confronted Evans about the previous murders, he "resolutely resisted that pressure" (para. 13) until undercover police officers unexpectedly took him to a correctional facility to visit an undercover officer posing as an attempted murderer. During a conversation with that operative, Evans disclosed that he himself had spent time in prison for murders he did not commit. The undercover operator laughed at him and sneeringly remarked that he didn't do it either, but went on to say, "I shanked her" (para. 13). Evans then responded that he had, in fact, killed the two girls. When asked if he had shot them, he replied, "No, I shanked them" (para. 13). Both victims, Lavonne Cheryl Willems and Beverly Seto, had in fact died as a result of multiple stab wounds (*Evans* 1988: paras. 68–69). Undercover officers maintained contact with their target and involved him in scenarios that ultimately led to considerable discussions about the possibility that Jake, an organizational member and hit man, might kill two people for Evans, an ex-girlfriend and the spouse of his current girlfriend (para. 15). Evans would eventually be charged with two counts of counselling murder.

Although chilling, the conversation related to the charge of counselling the murder of Evans' ex-girlfriend was not taken seriously because the undercover officers did not feel it was a serious threat (para. 28). As Mr. Justice Preston noted, in order to constitute a criminal offence, threats of death or serious bodily harm "must have been meant to be taken seriously" (para. 27). Consequently, Mr. Justice Preston acquitted Evans on the charge of counselling the murder of his ex-girlfriend. With respect to the charge of counselling the murder of David Williams, the spouse of Evan's girlfriend, Mr. Justice Preston found that Evans was serious when he instructed "Jake" to kill Mr. Williams (para. 30), but that based on the defence of entrapment set out in *Mack* (1988), the police "employed means which went further than providing an opportunity for Evans to commit the offence of counselling the murder of David Williams" (para. 34). Given that Evans was the subject of police entrapment, the appropriate remedy was a stay of proceedings (para. 36). In closing, Mr. Justice Preston proclaimed, "I should say that I found it difficult to believe that these events took place in Canada.... Undercover operations are very useful in police work. However, they do not allow the police to employ techniques that are antithetical to the principles of fairness embodied in the *Charter*" (para. 36).

Is an Admission from the Target Hearsay Governed by the Requirement for Necessity and Reliability?

Whether admissions are admissible under the traditional exception to the hearsay rule, or whether they are hearsay at all, is an area of law that is fraught with inconsistencies. In Canada, an out-of-court statement made by an accused person is, for the most part, admissible as evidence under the exception to the rule against hearsay (Brockman and Rose 2011: 218).

In 1990, the Supreme Court of Canada developed a principled approach to determining the admissibility of hearsay statements, an approach that requires the trial judge to ascertain whether necessity and reliability have been established (*Khan* 1990: para. 33; also see *Starr* 2000: para. 153). In *Hawkins* (1996: para. 75), the Supreme Court of Canada explained the nature of the analysis, stating that it is the role of the trial judge to determine whether the hearsay statement meets the criteria of necessity and threshold reliability, "so as to afford the trier of fact a satisfactory basis" for evaluating the truthfulness of the statement and the weight to be attached to it. Nowlin (2004) argues that inducements held out to Mr. Big targets raise serious doubt about the reliability of these confessions; this very factor, he claims, provides "the circumstances of *untrustworthiness* that should lead to the statement's exclusion according to *Starr*" (397).

In ten of eighty-one decisions, counsel for the accused challenged the admissibility of statements made to undercover operators, arguing that the statements were hearsay and required the application of necessity and reliability analysis of the principled exception to the hearsay rule. Two decisions (*Wytyshyn* 2002; and *Bridges* 2005) held that the threshold reliability test from the Starr analysis was applicable and then proceeded to find that threshold reliability was met. The remainder of the cases rejected the *Starr* analysis for admissions on the basis of Mr. Justice Sopinka's questioning of whether admissions are really an exception to the hearsay rule (*Evans* 1993: para. 24). These included, for example, *MacMillan* (2003a: para. 13), *Perovic* (2004a: para. 19), *Foreman* (2002: para. 32), *Lowe* (2004: para. 224), and *Ciancio* (2007: para. 16). The Ontario Court of Appeal in *Osmar* (2007a: para. 53), and the British Columbia Appellate Court in *Terrico*

(2005: para. 46–47) and *Bonisteel* (2008) concluded that the *Starr* analysis was not required. The position that the *Starr* analysis is not applicable is bolstered by the fact that the Supreme Court of Canada denied leave to appeal in *Terrico* even after Mme. Justice Newbury observed in *Terrico* (2005: para. 22) that this issue is one in "which the guidance of the highest court in Canada would be useful."

The Concern with False Confessions

In his reasons for judgment in *Perovic* (2004b: para. 26), Mr. Justice Williams acknowledged that the "carefully structured [Mr. Big] relationships provide substantial inducements to targets to make confessions to crimes and that they create very real concerns that false confessions may be offered." In addition, confessions are often the product of psychological manipulation and implied threats of physical harm, which unquestionably undermine their reliability. Mr. Justice Williams elaborated:

> I recognize that such undercover operations tend to encourage false bravado and boastfulness in the targets. There is a real concern that the targets will exaggerate their role in any activity. I am aware that the statements thus made are not contrary to the penal interest of the subject but, rather, occur in an atmosphere where there is a pressure upon the subject to claim credit for criminal activity. I recognize that the undercover operators often make generous payments to targets for their performance of apparent criminal activities, that they hold out a powerful inducement of membership in a sophisticated and wealthy organization, and that the target engages in dealings with individuals who are made to appear powerful and capable of great violence. (*Perovic* 2004b: para. 25)

It is disconcerting that a confession was vital evidence in the prosecution of twenty-three of these cases, given that social science research suggests that confession evidence has a significant biasing effect on jurors' perceptions and decision-making processes and that an admission of guilt alone can conceivably ensure a guilty verdict (Conti 1999; Driver 1968; Drizin and Leo 2004; Kassin and Sukel 1997; Kassin and Neumann 1997; Kassin and Wrightsman 1980, 1981; Leo and Ofshe 1998a; Wrightsman, Nietzel, and Fortune 1994). Nowlin's (2004) analysis of the Mr. Big post-offence undercover operation prompted him to ask why these apparent confessions are "presumed to have some air of reliability, sufficient to be put to the jury, instead of being presumed to be unreliable, at least without more" (Nowlin 2004: 395). Within the frame work of the current Canadian criminal justice system, no legal safeguards or mechanisms are in place to regularly challenge the reliability of a suspect's out-of-court statement in a Mr. Big operation.

Should the trial judge, in his or her charge to the jury, be required to instruct the jury specifically as to the unreliability of an accused's admissions to undercover police officers, "in accordance with obiter dicta in R. v. Hodgson [1998] 2 S.C.R. 449" (Terrico 2005: para. 3)? The British Columbia Court of Appeal has delivered seven judgments, and the Ontario Court of Appeal one judgment, related specifically to this issue. In all eight cases, the appellate courts upheld the trial judge's decision not to give the jury a specific direction concerning the inherent unreliability of the accused's statements to undercover police.[4]

Despite assertions from Brian Carter that he was "extremely frightened at the time he made the statement" to the undercover officers and that their interrogation tactics created "an atmosphere calculated to strike fear and to completely overrun any resistance or choice that a person may want to exercise" (Carter 2001: para. 27), Mme. Justice Ryan concluded that a "Hodgson warning" about the reliability of Carter's confession to the undercover police officers was not necessary. Mirroring this sentiment, Mme. Justice McFadyen, for the majority in Grandinetti (2003: para. 27), ruled that since there was no air of reality to an allegation that the appellants' statements were made in oppressive or threatening circumstances, a specific warning from the trial judge was not necessary. More recently, in Osmar (2007a), Mr. Justice Rosenberg affirmed the order of the Ontario Superior Court of Justice that a "Hodgson warning" would have been of no assistance to the appellant. While there were inducements offered to Osmar, Mr. Justice Rosenberg observed, "his treatment by the undercover officers that led to the confession could not be properly characterized as degrading and did not include the use of violence or threats of violence" (para. 76).

Despite these rulings, the appellate courts have also made it clear that statements made during the course of a Mr. Big undercover sting operation should be viewed as inherently unreliable; they should be scrutinized with extreme care and hold little or no probative value unless confirmed by other independent evidence (Bonisteel 2008; Forknall 2003; G.W.F. 2003; McCreery 1998; Skiffington 2004; Terrico 2005). But a review of these authorities suggests that there is no "specific formulation of a warning that must be given" as it relates to the reliability of the statements made by the accused to undercover police officers (see McCreery 1998: para. 26; Bonisteel 2008: para. 73).

Gudjonsson (2003b: 582) theorizes that admitting confessions obtained through a Mr. Big scenario into evidence, and letting a jury determine their probative value, is worrying "because the risk of such confessions being false is considerable if an innocent person is coerced in this way." In fact, he contends that the possibility of eliciting a false confession could be even greater in this noncustodial context. Unlike the situation in custodial interrogation settings, targets of the Mr. Big scenarios do not perceive the potentially devastating consequences of confessing to a crime. They might offer up unreliable, misleading, or erroneous statements merely as a way of compromising between agreeing to something they did not do (i.e. telling lies about the involvement in the offence) and fear of the consequences if they do not confess (i.e. perceived certainty of a conviction, upsetting the members of the organization with whom they have developed a relationship and being rejected by the criminal organization). (582)

Correspondingly, social psychologist Dr. Richard Ofshe, a leading expert on the phenomenon of false confessions, agues that the Mr. Big undercover operation is "a potentially dangerous one because there is no downside to making the claim of involvement in criminality" (*Osmar* 2007a: para. 60). Ofshe testified, in a *voir dire* to determine the admissibility of evidence in *Osmar* (2007a), that in this type of undercover investigation, "the possibility of being punished for confessing falls to zero since the suspect perceives the situation as one in which the state is not involved" (para. 60).

In *Mentuck* (2000b: para. 100), Mr. Justice MacInnes cautioned the police to "be aware that as the level of inducement increases, the risk of receiving a confession to an offence which one did not commit increases, and the reliability of the confession diminishes correspondingly." In *Ciancio* (2006: para. 273), Mme. Justice Boyd was of the view that "an overly generous offer may induce the target to make untruthful statements in order to be part of the organization."

Dr. Shabehram Lohrasbe, a forensic psychologist with special expertise in the area of false confessions, testified in *C.K.R.S.* (2005) that a suspect's economic status could increase the likelihood of giving erroneous information to police, and could, therefore, play a role in eliciting a false confession (para. 93, 95).[5] This connection is particularly relevant, since many of the targets of Mr. Big scenarios are marginalized persons "on the fringes" of society (Baron 2008a: A.4).[6] Their status may seriously undermine the reliability of these supposed admissions. Thus, the question becomes how to delicately balance an opportunity structure so as not compromise the reliability of the statements or even worse, elicit a false confession or admission (Nowlin 2004: 394).

Techniques to Enhance the Reliability of Disclosures

The RCMP has acknowledged that undercover operations compromise the reliability of statements made by targets, and that the Mr. Big technique could potentially encourage a suspect to intentionally overestimate his or her participation and culpability in the alleged offence (Baron 2008a; Ciancio 2006: para. 169; Henry 2003: para. 44). A B.C. lawyer who represents the RCMP explained the need to offset potential fallibilities: "We know a lot of these individuals are not the sharpest knives in the drawer. We can exploit their naiveté to get to the truth. But what we have to be careful about is that we do get to the truth" (Baron 2008a: A4). The RCMP maintains that it has developed mechanisms to discourage falsification or even fabrication of statements, and "ensure the utterances obtained from an accused are reliable" (*Ciancio* 2006: para. 268). While this is a laudable goal, there is some question as to whether these techniques actually ensure the reliability of an accused's assertions.

The participants in Mr. Big stings are, by and large, undercover police officers. On occasion, the police have employed informants in their investigations. In *Joseph* (2000a) and *Mentuck* (2000b), informants were used primarily as proxies to introduce targets to the primary undercover police officer. In *Ciancio* (2006), the RCMP hired a career criminal and associate of the target, Robert Moyes, as an informant and as an agent. Due to the unique circumstances of the case, the undercover officers "were forced to rely on what was assumed to be an established and solid relationship" between Moyes (an informant) and the target (para. 269). Regarding the credibility and reliability of Moyes, Mme. Justice Boyd stated:

> To say that Moyes is a career criminal falls far short of describing him. He became a heroin addict in his early teens. Approximately 35 of his 50 years have been spent in jail. During that period he has followed a well established pattern of successfully deceiving, manipulating, and lying to his treating psychologists, substance abuse counsellors, social workers, and parole officers and other prison authorities, thus earning their trust and a repeated "cascading down" of security levels within the corrections system. Following his well established pattern, once outside in the community, he has regularly breached that trust by abusing drugs and alcohol and very quickly returning to violent criminal activity. (para. 19)

In her decision, Mme. Justice Boyd acknowledged the inherent difficulties of eliciting self-incriminating statements from the accused (para. 289). Nonetheless, while Ciancio's assertions were "consistent with him at least knowing about the murders," he disclosed nothing that was "particularly revealing or surprising" (para. 279). What's more, Mme. Justice Boyd found no independent evidence to corroborate the informant's version of events (para. 289). As a result, she ruled that the Crown failed to prove its case beyond a reasonable doubt, and the accused was acquitted of two counts of first-degree murder.

Baron (2008a) reports that the Mr. Big technique originated in the early 1990s, when an RCMP undercover police officer was investigating a murder and used a civilian agent to gather evidence (A4). That undercover operation is said to have failed, and the crime remains unsolved. The officer recalled, "I thought, 'Why do we have to involve that third party? Why can't we go out and get it ourselves'" (Baron 2008a: A4). Most Mr. Big operations take place with undercover police officers forming relationships with the targets and gathering evidence. Informants seem to be used only when the undercover police officers are unable to make the connections.

Adherence to the Code of Trust, Honesty and Loyalty

Undercover operators befriend the target and gradually gain his or her confidence through a series of scenarios, creating a "carefully structured relationship" (*Perovic* 2004: para. 26). A fundamental theme that resonates throughout the operation is the adherence to "the code" of honesty, reliability, and loyalty, the "fundamental tenets of the organization" (*Wilson* 2007: para. 83). In *Lowe* (2004), Mme. Justice C.L. Smith considered the significance of these themes, observing that, "The homilies about the importance of honesty and coming clean with the boss were on occasion backed up by exemplary tales" (para. 236). Undercover operatives stage unpleasant scenarios to show what happens to individuals who deceive, cheat, or lie to the organization. Moreover, Mr. Big cautions that he will use his "sources" (e.g., reliable information from a police source) to inquire into the veracity of the target's statements. The bottom line, according to the police, is that targets are made well aware of, and understand, the consequences of dishonesty.

Holdback Evidence and Its Contamination

For tactical reasons, investigators intentionally withhold specific elements of the crime, "evidence that only the actual killer could be expected to know" (*Fliss* 2002: para. 58). Known as holdback evidence, these particulars help test the validity of the confession (*Black* 2007: para. 630). This deliberate safeguard is, according to an RCMP lawyer, "the finest litmus test out there" to ensure that any potential disclosures by the target are not undermined by suggestions or leading questions from interrogators, and to preserve the integrity and trustworthiness of statements (Baron 2008a: A4; *Griffin* 2001a: para. 34; *MacMillan* 2000: para. 23).

Contamination of holdback evidence in criminal investigation, however, is insidious. Contamination is the process whereby a suspect acquires special knowledge of a criminal event that is known only to the true perpetrator and/or the police (Leo and Ofshe 1998: 438). Indeed, such knowledge of a criminal event can be obtained through a variety of sources, including the media, the police, crime scene visits, crime scene materials (e.g., photographs), and details provided by a third party; during questioning, an interrogator may reveal facts about the crime disclosed by the real perpetrator; in the case of smaller towns, information may circulate through community channels (Gudjonsson 2003b: 180; Leo and Ofshe 1998a: 438).

As stated earlier, undercover police officers elicited a confession from Patrick Fischer by suggesting that Mr. Big could hire an expert to help him beat a polygraph examination. Mr. Justice Hall, in writing the decision of the British Columbia Court of Appeal, stated:

> Unfortunately for the appellant, the evidence developed against him by the undercover operation was powerful. He gave to [UC1] a wealth of detail about the homicide only the actual killer of Ms. Drefko could know. The site he pointed out to [UC2] was a near perfect match of the location where the

body was discovered, which is particularly damning because Fischer told the officers he placed the body in that location in the dark. (*Fischer* 2005: para. 55)

To recapitulate, the police withheld information related to the area where the body was located, and the fact that the cause of death was manual strangulation (*Fischer* 2005: para. 2). Given that the deceased's body was found on May 15, 1999 and that the undercover operation commenced a year later, is it possible that the holdback evidence Fischer disclosed to undercover operators was compromised? There was considerable opportunity for contamination. Concerning the location of the body, the sixteen-year-old girl's remains were discovered not by police, but by a group of eleven horseback riders from the lower mainland. Upon returning to the ranch, they informed the owner's sixteen-year-old son of their gruesome discovery, gave him directions, and asked him to contact the police. Linda Fischer, Patrick's mother, stated that on May 15, 1999, at least twenty local high school students attended what is colloquially known as "GangBang Flats" for a pre-graduation party, many of them camping on Lilly Lake Road near the site where the body was found. At trial, four individuals testified to having seen the police cars as they were heading to the party. The following day, a helicopter was seen hovering over the site. In the days following the discovery of the body, the local newspaper, the *Merritt Herald*, ran a front-page story revealing the location of the body. Mrs. Fischer claims that at least thirty-two people knew that Drefko's body was located in a wooded area off Lilly Lake road (*Fischer* 2006).

During the undercover operation, Fischer took one undercover officer to a location where he said he dumped the body. The British Columbia Court of Appeal noted, "This was not the precise location where the body had been discovered but it was less than 100 yards from the site. Fischer had pointed out a log to F. and the body was discovered by the riders near a log" (2005: para. 20).

No one had been told directly that strangulation was the cause of death, the RCMP interview with the sister of the deceased, Susan, discussed the subject of "sleepers" (*Fischer* 2005: para. 4). Linda Fischer describes sleepers as a game "where pressure is applied to the major artery in the neck and people pass out and get a bit of a high" (*Fischer* 2006). At trial, the accused testified that, following a conversation with Susan, he concluded that strangulation was the cause of death (2005: para. 39).

Apart from Fischer's confession to the RCMP, there was no physical or forensic evidence linking Fischer to the murder (para. 18). Is it possible that Fischer was able to piece together a persuasive story based on news media accounts and what others had told him? On November 30, 2001, a jury convicted Patrick Fischer of the first-degree murder of Darci Drefko. The British Columbia Court of Appeal found no merit to his claims that he fabricated the story to impress the undercover officers, and dismissed his appeal from conviction. Finally, on further appeal to the Supreme Court of Canada, his application for leave to appeal was dismissed without reasons. The appeals process is exhausted, and yet questions remain about the veracity of his admissions to undercover police. Presently, Fischer's case is being reviewed by AIDWYC.

In some cases, the police limit the amount of information the operative has about the crime and the target in order to reduce the danger of contamination. In *C.K.R.S.* (2005), for example, the primary undercover operator posing as the main contact for the criminal organization was given a brief fact sheet containing minimal information. The fact sheet stated, in part, that the "Investigation reveals that C.K.R.S. is currently living in the Eastside area of Vancouver. C.K.R.S. is believed to be unemployed. He is also considered to be a violent individual and an abuser of alcohol and narcotics. C.K.R.S. has an extensive criminal record dating back to 1960" (para. 32). Similarly, in *Griffin* (2001), the primary undercover operator was given minimal information about the target and the investigation. Although she was told that the investigation related to a twenty-year-old homicide, she knew nothing else about the alleged crime: not the cause of death, the location of the body, or the relationship, if any, between the accused and the deceased (*Griffin* 2001: para. 34).[7]

In only twelve of the eighty-one cases reviewed did it appear that, in their confessions to undercover operatives, the accused disclosed details held back from press releases.[8] While the disclosure of holdback evidence increases the trustworthiness of a self-incriminating statement, the discovery of incriminating evidence previously unknown to police (e.g., leading police to missing evidence) further strengthens the validity of a confession (Gudjonsson 2003b: 131). In another eleven cases, the suspect disclosed information that was unknown to police. The case of *McCreery* (1998a) demonstrates how the Mr. Big undercover strategy was able to unearth such previously unknown evidence. On August 15, 1994, Landis Heal's former common-law spouse called police to file a missing persons report on him (para. 5). In early October, the RCMP discovered the victim's vehicle abandoned in the bush, but were still unable to locate the victim. Following a number of tips, the RCMP mounted an undercover operation against Timothy McCreery in an attempt to determine if he was involved criminally in the victim's death (para. 7). In the course of the undercover operation, the accused and the primary undercover operator were to attend a meeting with Mr. Big at a local hotel. Just before the interview, the operative told McCreery to be completely honest with the boss, who might hire him (para. 11). Not only did McCreery inform Mr. Big that he had in fact killed Heal, but later that evening, he directed undercover officers to the victim's body, which was subsequently recovered as evidence (para. 12). Nevertheless, in any of the cases with evidence or previously unknown evidence, a target's knowledge of the evidence is not necessarily conclusive of his or her guilt. The target could have acquired the information through other avenues.

Clandestine Audio and Video Recording

Audio and videorecording is one method of assisting the trier of fact in deciding the credibility of confessions made during Mr. Big operations. The undercover investigation often culminates in a lengthy meeting between Mr. Big and the target, akin to a job interview, regarding the target's future in the criminal organization (*Bicknell* 2003: para. 103). The target is asked about his or her involvement in the crime under investigation, questions that generally result in inculpatory admissions from the suspect (*Peterffy* 2000: para. 6). These meetings, which are often surreptitiously videotaped and audiotaped (pursuant to judicial authorization), are usually held in hotel rooms because of the ease in equipping the room with surveillance equipment, and also because members of the investigative team can monitor the meetings and surveillance equipment from adjacent rooms (*C.K.R.S.* 2005: para. 41). They are prepared to move in immediately if things go awry. RCMP Supt. Lorne Schwartz admitted, "violence is rare, but it happens" (Baron 2004b: A8).[9] Where possible, and pursuant to judicial authorization, police will install recording devices in safe houses and vehicles (Mentuck 2000b; *United States of America v. Burns* 1997) and other more secretive locations (for example, see *Aubee* 2006: para. 20).

In fifty-two of eighty-one cases, the videotaped conversations, as well as supplementary transcripts of the exchanges between the accused and Mr. Big, were admitted into evidence at trial and put before the trier of fact. Videotaped recordings and transcripts might have been used in additional cases, but this information was not available in the material accessed by the researchers. According to Trotter (2004), the advantages that result from recording in custody interrogations can be categorized as epistemological, behavioural, and systemic (para. 48). The same advantages apply to recording Mr. Big scenarios. From an epistemological standpoint, a videotaped record of the conversations between law enforcement officers and suspects provides an objective and authentic account of all that transpired during the interview/interrogation, which helps to counteract forgetfulness and self-serving distortions in memory (Trotter 2004: para. 49; Kassin 2005: 225). Although detailed note-taking by officers may capture the essence of what occurred, a video recording "preserves and conveys both the tone in which words were uttered and the body language of those present" (Trotter 2004: para. 49). As Mr. Justice Iacobucci pointed out in *Oickle* (2000: para. 46), a recorded interrogation is of great value to a judge and/ or jury as it provides them a means by which they can evaluate the reliability of the suspect's confession, and thus decide how much probative value to attribute to it. For example, in *Grandinetti* (2003: para. 44), the trial judge found that the accused's demeanour on the recordings was inconsistent with the suggestion that he was being intimidated. As noted by Mr. Justice J.W. Williams in *Perovic* (2004a: para. 77), "The Court's opportunity to understand and appreciate the actual atmosphere in the interview and the nuances of the exchange is enormously enhanced by the fact that a videotape of the entire event was available."

From a behavioural perspective, the police will be more likely to conduct themselves in a professional manner and will be less likely to employ questionable interrogation practices under the gaze of a camera (Trotter 2004: para. 51). Videotaping thus protects the rights of the accused. At the same time, such recordings also shield the police from frivolous claims of police misconduct (Kassin 2005: 225; Trotter 2004: para. 51; White 1997: 154).

Lastly, Trotter (2004) argues that the videotaping of police interviews and interrogations systemically buttresses the overall reputation of the criminal justice system, increasing and/or restoring confidence in the administration of justice (para. 52). The electronic recording of all police interviews and interrogations allows the public to examine what has typically been a behind-closed-doors process (Gudjonsson 2003b: 22). As Mr. Justice Iacobucci, for the majority in *Oickle* (2001), stated, the law "cannot countenance secrecy" (para. 46).

Although not yet required by law, commentators in the area agree on the need for a policy that mandates the videotaping of all interviews and interrogations (Cassell 1996a: 1996b, 1999; Conti 1999; Drizin and Colgan 2001; Drizin and Leo 2004; Gohara 2006; Gudjonsson 1992, 2003b; Inbau et al. 1986; Johnson 1997; Kassin 2005; Kassin and Gudjonsson 2004; Leo 2005; Leo and Ofshe 1998b; Loewy 2007; Marx 1988; Ofshe and Leo 1997b; Penney 2004; Sangero 2007; Silbey 2006; Soree 2005; Thurlow 2005; Trotter 2004; White 1997). The same arguments can be made for recording interrogations in Mr. Big investigations, and indeed, the culminating confession in a Mr. Big scenario is often videotaped. However, much of the grooming and socialization of targets into the criminal organization is not recorded.

The Honourable Mr. Justice Cory, in the commission of inquiry into the wrongful conviction of Thomas Sophonow, identified several disquieting, multi-faceted errors penetrating all levels of the criminal justice system that led to Sophonow's wrongful conviction and imprisonment. In his report, Mr. Justice Cory took issue with the manner in which Sophonow was interrogated. In addition to questioning Sophonow for prolonged periods of time, the two interrogating officers did not properly transcribe the interrogation, which led to serious discrepancies between what Sophonow said to investigators and what the investigators reported (Cory 2001). As a result, Mr. Justice Cory made the following recommendations urging the video recording of all police interrogations:

> The evidence pertaining to statements given by an accused will always be of great importance in a trial. The possibility of errors occurring in manually transcribing a verbal statement by anyone other than a skilled shorthand reporter is great; the possibility of misinterpreting the words of the accused is great; and the possibility of abusive procedures, although slight, exists in those circumstances. That, coupled with the ease with which a tape recording can be made, make it necessary to exclude unrecorded statements of an

accused. It is the only sure means of avoiding the admission of inaccurate, misinterpreted and false statements.

I would recommend that videotaping of interviews with suspects be made a rule and an adequate explanation given before the audiotaping of an interview is accepted as admissible. This is to say, all interviews must be videotaped or, at the very least, audiotaped.

Further, interviews that are not taped should, as a general rule, be inadmissible. There is too great a danger in admitting oral statements. They are not verbatim and are subject to misinterpretation and errors, particularly of omission. Their dangers are too many and too serious to permit admission. Tape recorders are sufficiently inexpensive and accessible that they can be provided to all investigating officers and used to record the statements of any suspect. (Cory 2001)

Although some of these techniques may decrease the possibility of false confessions, Mr. Big scenarios have the additional problem of painting their targets with a criminal brush. Evidence that the targets are interested in acting for a criminal organization and the activities they carry out to prove themselves to the fake criminal organization provide negative evidence of their character and point to predispositions towards crime.

Narrative Evidence Tends to Show Bad Character or a Criminal Disposition

As a general rule, evidence of an accused's unrelated past activity is subject to a general exclusionary rule because it has been shown to have a highly prejudicial effect on juries, and there is "considerable danger that it will be used illogically or given too much weight" (Sopinka et al. 1999: 472; also see Brockman and Rose 2011: 281).[10] In seventeen cases, counsel for the accused challenged the trial judge's decision to admit the accused's confession in evidence, arguing that evidence of the accused's bad character was "inextricably bound up" with the confession to undercover police officers and therefore highly prejudicial and otherwise irrelevant to the prosecution's case. Admission of such evidence raised concerns that the jury, when assessing the testimonial trustworthiness of the accused, would give it more weight than was warranted (see *Caster* 1998; *G. (S.G.)* 1997; *Redd* 2002). In all but one case, however, the trial judge ruled the statements admissible as evidence.

That one case concerned Wesley Creek's post-undercover operation narrative. Subsequent to a *voir dire* held to determine its admissibility, Mr. Justice Stewart agreed with the submission of counsel for Creek that the prejudicial effects of Creek's statements to police, taken as a whole, far outweighed the potential probative value. He favoured the exclusion of the evidence over a limiting instruction to the jury because he believed a "prophylactic warning" would not counterbalance the prejudice of extrinsic misconduct (*Creek* 1998: para. 36). Moreover, Creek did not disclose information that the police held back from the public, and there was no other independent, reliable evidence to corroborate his statements. In the end, the statement was "not of great probative value" (*Creek* 1998: para. 33).

Although Mr. Justice Stewart's line of reasoning makes intuitive sense, his decision seems to be a legal anomaly. Yet as Nowlin (2004: 383) points out, the circumstances of the Mr. Big undercover operation initiated against Creek are "not readily distinguishable" from that of other cases. As a matter of policy, Nowlin (2004) recommends that "in the absence of cogent, corroborative, real or circumstantial evidence" that enhances the reliability of confessions made to Mr. Big, a general exclusionary rule should prevail (401).

Indeed, the social and economic incentives offered to targets (i.e., the promise of wealth and membership into a powerful criminal organization) can encourage "false bravado and boastfulness" (*Perovic* 2004b: para. 25) not only of an accused person's participation in the crime under investigation, but also of prior misconduct and criminal proclivity (Nowlin 2004: 395). According to Nowlin (2004),

> These cases speak more loudly about the willingness of some people to fabricate criminal histories about themselves for the sake of belonging to a powerful social group and acquiring real wealth illicitly than to the volumes of psychological studies and reported cases about false confessions elicited through police interrogation. (394)

The very fact that the target is seeking membership in what he or she believes to be a criminal organization speaks of his or her character in a negative way (*Raza* 1998: para. 81). As Mr. Justice Stewart observed in *Creek* (1998), "The dynamics set in motion by the undercover officers who presented themselves to the accused as hard core, successful and violent criminals was based on a perverted moral compass. That is to say, the worse the accused said of himself and his deeds, the better his future with the bad guys' criminal organization would be" (*Creek* 1998: para. 24). Targets have to demonstrate that they too are hardened criminals who can be trusted and are capable of "carrying out the kind of criminal acts required by the organization," even if it means falsifying or even concocting ostentatious stories of past criminal conduct (*Osmar* 2007a: para. 1).

Although highly prejudicial and otherwise irrelevant to the prosecution's case (not to mention contrary to jurisprudence relating to this area of the law), Canadian courts now admit evidence of an accused's bad character obtained as a result of a Mr. Big scenario. Mme. Justice McFadyen, for the majority in *Grandinetti* (2003), explained the rationale for this: it is "relevant to understanding the investigation and the context within which the conversations with the undercover police officers occurred" (para. 66) (see also Nowlin 2004: 381). A suspect's confession to undercover police officers is "inextricably interwoven" (*Bonisteel* 2008: para. 29) within the context of discussions relating to other criminal activities, be it prior misconduct and/or a willingness to engage in ongoing or future criminality (*Caster* 1998: para. 6).

Editing the Statements to Remove Prejudicial References?

As the Supreme Court of Canada observed in *Beatty v. the King* (1944), it is acceptable for the trial judge to edit the statements of an accused, removing irrelevant facts, if it can be done "without in any way affecting the tenor of it" (para. 3). Editing the undercover operation narrative to remove references to bad character, according to Nowlin (2004), is a "catch-22" and could be detrimental to an accused's case because the discussions relating to other criminal activities are often necessary to demonstrate that the so-called confession "is both incredible and unreliable," and that the confession was concocted to secure significant financial payments and membership in the fictitious criminal organization (402). In essence, Nowlin argues that the highly prejudicial and otherwise irrelevant evidence of bad character is necessary to the accused's defence (406).

In the rare event that a trial judge allows for editing of Mr. Big narratives, the editing is rather minimal. In *Caster*, for example, the trial judge allowed the excision of a discussion about whether a proposed murder in Edmonton should be a "closed or open casket" because it was "unnecessary and inflammatory to the narrative" (1998: para. 31). However, other discussions about the proposed murder were not excised. The trial judge explained that "the jury can be expressly instructed to consider the Edmonton proposal evidence as a contextual lead-in to Caster's eventual admissions and not as evidence of a general propensity on his part to kill others" (para. 29).

Unless there are unusual circumstances, the Canadian judiciary has steered clear of editing the accused's statements to undercover police officers because these statements ostensibly provide "some apparently relevant 'narrative' or synonymous notion such as 'context'" (Nowlin 2004: 412). Mr. Justice Parrett, in *Cretney*, cautioned that abridged statements might result in a "form of manufactured circumstances substantially altered from reality" (1999: para. 32). Although evidence of the accused's discreditable conduct incidentally demonstrates bad character, Parrett observed, his statements to undercover police officers were both relevant and necessary to the truthfulness of the accused's confession, "and essential to a fair unfolding of the narrative and to enable the jury to have a full and proper understanding of the circumstances in which the statements were made" (*Cretney* 1999: para. 33).

Instructions to the Jury

The appellate courts delivered judgment in eight of the eighty-one cases concerning a limiting instruction to the jury about the use of character evidence. The thrust of the argument raised on appeal was that the trial judge erred in failing to sufficiently instruct the jury about drawing adverse inferences against the accused because of his or her participation in the criminal enterprise. In her instructions to the jury concerning the improper use of this evidence, the trial judge in *Grandinetti* (2003) stated:

You must not, and I stress the word must not infer from this evidence of character and disposition alone that Cory Grandinetti was a person likely to have committed the offence of murder. In other words, you cannot use this evidence or consider this evidence for the purpose of proving that the accused is a person who by reason of his criminal character or propensity is likely to have committed the crime charged. (*Grandinetti* 2003: para. 72)

Mme. Justice McFadyen, for the majority of the Alberta Court of Appeal, found that both the limiting instructions and the timing of those instructions sufficiently addressed the issue that the jury might have drawn improper inferences about the accused. She was confident, moreover, that members of the jury were sufficiently competent and intelligent to comprehend the trial judge's warning (para. 73).

Vincent Redd argued unsuccessfully that his involvement in what he believed to be criminal conduct, as well as admissions to undercover operatives regarding previous criminal conduct, was not relevant to any issue in his case and ought to have been excluded (*Redd* 2002: para. 35). In his undercover narrative he not only claimed responsibility for the murder of Keitha Llewellyn, the victim of the homicide charge before the court, but also admitted to the shooting of Gerard Hurley in Chiliwack, B.C., and to four other homicides in Alberta which police investigated and determined to be conjured up (para. 159; see also Nowlin 2004: 403). The trial judge, Mme. Justice Saunders, ruled that the probative value of this evidence outweighed its prejudicial effect and that Redd's statements had "sufficient imprimatur of reliability to go to the jury" (para. 172). In her limiting instruction to the jury on the use of this evidence, she stated, "The reason this evidence was allowed was as part of the narrative and to provide a full picture for you, including not just of Mr. Redd, but also of the two undercover officers as that may relate to your assessment of credibility" (*Redd* 2002: para. 41). She advised that jurors "should disregard any evidence relating to the character or disposition of Mr. Redd that showed he was involved in immoral, or illegal activities and, most specifically, you must not infer from this evidence of character or disposition that Mr. Redd was a person likely to have committed the killing of Keitha Llewellyn" (*Redd* 2002: para. 41).

In *Bonisteel* (2008), the appellant submitted that, in addition to other prejudicial matters, the trial judge erred by not removing references to Bonisteel's previous rape convictions, which were irrelevant and highly prejudicial (para. 28). It was argued that the "extreme prejudice posed by the evidence could not be ameliorated by jury instructions" (para. 28). The trial judge concluded that the prejudicial portions of Bonisteel's statements were inextricably interwoven with, and relevant to, the truthfulness of the confession (para. 48). The majority decision of the British Columbia Court of Appeal, written by Mme. Justice Levine, found that the trial judge did not err in his limiting instructions to the jury, nor was he required to edit the accused's statements.

The rationale for allowing out-of-court statements to be admitted as evidence is based on the assumption that a "prophylactic warning to the jury" (*Creek* 1998: para. 36) on the prohibited use of this type of evidence will prevent the jury from drawing any adverse inferences against the accused (*B. (F.F.)* 1993: para. 80; *G. (S.G.)* 1997: para. 72). In *W. (D.)* (1991), Mr. Justice Cory, for the majority, was confident that jurors are able to understand and follow the trial judge's instructions: "Today's jurors are intelligent and conscientious, anxious to perform their duties as jurors in the best possible manner. They are not likely to be forgetful of instructions" (761).

Despite the judiciary's confidence in jurors' ability to understand legal instructions, an overwhelming number of social scientific studies draw the conclusion that jurors have difficulty comprehending and following legal instructions (Cutler and Hughes 2001; Jackson 1992; Jones and Myers 1979; Reifman, Gusick, and Ellsworth 1992; Rose 2003; Rose and Ogloff 2001; Saxton 1998; Severance and Loftus 1982, 1984; Severance, Greene, and Loftus 1984; Young, Cameron, and Tinsley 2001). Dufraimont (2008) suggests that miscarriages of justice resulting from unreliable evidence are most acute in jury trials. Unfamiliar with the criminal justice system and inexperienced in criminal law, lay jurors do not normally possess the requisite knowledge or skills to properly evaluate evidence tendered at trial, and "can be led astray by common sense beliefs that are misguided" (2008: para. 3).

Concern about jurors' overvaluation of character evidence is supported by early jury simulation research, which has shown that disclosure of a suspect's prior criminal record causes jurors to form an unfavourable opinion of the accused; this opinion inexorably influences their decision of guilt or innocence. In fact, jurors who possess information about the accused's prior criminal record are more likely to convict than jurors who have no information, and the judge's limiting instructions on the use of criminal record evidence have been shown to have little effect on jurors' determination of guilt or innocence (Doob and Kirshenbaum 1972; Hans and Doob 1976; Sealy and Cornish 1973). More recent simulation experiments have corroborated previous findings that limiting instructions on the use of criminal record evidence are ineffective in preventing jurors from using that evidence when determining guilt or innocence (Greene and Dodge 1995; Rose 2003; Wissler, Kuehn, and Saks 2000).

A number of studies have been conducted in which people who had previously served on juries in criminal trials were asked whether the trial judge's instructions were helpful to them (Cutler and Hughes 2001; Jackson 1992; Reifman, Gusick, and Ellsworth 1992; Saxton 1998; Young, Cameron, and Tinsley 2001). In all studies, most jurors asserted a high level of comprehension, finding that the trial judge's instructions were clear, easy to understand, and helpful to them in their task. Despite jurors' confidence in having understood the trial judge's instructions, however, "their confidence is not a good measure of actual understanding, which was found to be significantly lower than the participants had believed" (Ogloff and Rose 2005: 412). Juror comprehension studies within the context of a simulated trial (i.e., mock jury paradigm) have also confirmed the supposition that jurors not only have difficulty comprehending and following judicial instructions, they also have a limited understanding of the law (Jones and Myers 1979; Rose and Ogloff 2001; Severance and Loftus 1984).

While the Supreme Court of Canada has advanced a general exclusionary rule to address the issues associated with character evidence in other cases, the admission of character evidence (in the disguise of narrative evidence) in Mr. Big investigations needs the Court's attention.

Rewriting the Criminal Law to Accommodate Mr. Big

Although section 25.1 of the *Criminal Code* now provides a framework that "allows police officers to break the law under limited circumstances with the permission of their superiors" (Brockman and Rose 2011: 231), Mr. Big investigations appear to rely on the proposition that the undercover officers' make-believe crimes do not have the requisite *mens rea* to fall under the definitions of criminal offences (see Gorbet 2004 referred to in Chapter 1). In some cases, this requires a creative interpretation of the law; in other cases, creative interpretation is not sufficient to bring the behaviour of the police outside the scope of the criminal law.

For example, in *Forknall* (2000: para. 16), the accused argued that his *Charter* rights were violated by the fact that undercover police officers engaged in forgery (contrary to section 366 of the *Criminal Code*), intimidation (section 423), uttered a forged document (section 368), and uttered threats (section 264). The trial judge found that because the documents were police documents, there was no forgery. With regard to the fact that the documents were not an extract from the PIRS system, he found that the "statement was made orally and not directly in the document itself" (para. 17).

On the allegation of uttering threats, the trial judge had to be slightly more creative. Although Forknall might "reasonably have inferred from [UC1's] comments about getting 'whacked' (killed), and 'he kicks my ass once I kick your ass twice' and similar statements" that he might at some time be at the receiving end of violence from the criminal organization he was trying to join, there were no direct threats (para. 18). In addition, the words "were not spoken with the intent to intimidate and cause fear, but with the intent to convince the accused that the undercover operation really was a criminal operation; accordingly the threats were not uttered as threats" (para. 20). The trial judge did concede that if the words had been intended as threats, rather than deception, the undercover officers would have committed offences (para. 20). Though the threats may not have been technically a criminal offence (although one could argue that the undercover police officers intended to threaten and intimidate the target and that their motive — which is irrelevant — was to deceive), the distinction is probably lost on others charged with uttering threats and on the public more generally.

In *Cretney* (1999: para. 15) alcohol was made readily available to Cretney, who was a struggling alcoholic. According to the trial judge, one of the under-cover officers testified that the purpose of using alcohol "was to add realism to their contacts and to convince the accused that if he [the undercover officer] was prepared to drink and drive he was obviously not a police officer" (para. 15). The trial judge dismissed the accused's argument that the undercover officers' behav-iour undermined the integrity of the judicial process and found that "that the use of alcohol in this investigation was nothing more than a prop which provided a part of the 'entry point' for [the undercover officer] and a significant measure of protection for the officer by building his cover and credibility" (para. 28). The trial judge appears to endorse a rather broad scope of behaviour:

> It is neither logical nor required in law that police officers investigating seri-ous offences such as murder seek to convert their targets from their normal activities to afternoon tea and contract bridge parties. Indeed, what will normally be required if undercover operations are to enjoy some opportunity for success is for the officer to seek to participate in the normal activities of the target. (para. 29)

In *Joseph* (2000a), the trial judge had to deal with numerous allegations of criminal offences committed by the undercover operatives. Mr. Justice Taylor found that:

> In terms of the transport of supposed narcotics, counting of the purported proceeds of crime, threatening a reluctant payor, and scouting out of landing sites for drug shipments, it should not be forgotten that each of these were elaborate ruses: no narcotics, no stolen goods or proceeds of crime were actu-ally involved, nor any landing ever intended. (2000a: para. 69)

Mr. Justice Taylor also dismissed the argument that the police were illegally offer-ing to provide the accused with an alibi because they had no intentions to actually do so (para. 72–75). In examining the illegal transportation of weapons, he found that the police did engage in unlawfully assisting the target to commit an offence and were parties to the offence (para. 70, 83); however, such behaviour was not sufficient to "shock the conscience of the community," a measure that would have required its exclusion (para. 89).

The Supreme Court of Canada has strongly condemned illegal behaviour by the police even if it is for the purpose of law enforcement. In *Campbell*, the Court commented that "breaking a law in order to better enforce it has important rami-fications for the rule of law" (1999: para. 19). The court explained that "a crucial element of the rule of law is that '[t]here is ... one law for all'" (para. 18). In light of the Supreme Court of Canada's pronouncement, the condoning of criminal conduct by the police leads to serious questions about how the judiciary have been taken in by the "success" of some Mr. Big investigations.

Mr. Big Leads to Moral Decay

Despite its seeming success in some cases, we must consider the morally troubling costs of this interrogation technique, and whether it exceeds professional and ethical boundaries. Undercover operatives in a Mr. Big investigation use public funds to engage in, or stage, criminal activities. In addition, they subsidize numerous costs including transportation (business-class air travel), quartering themselves and targets in some of Canada's finest hotels, and dining at some of this country's most lavish restaurants; depending on the target's lifestyle choices, they might treat targets to activities such as watching exotic dancers (Baron 2008a: A4).

The discourse that undercover officers engage in encourages some of their targets to believe that women and children play a subordinate and often freely accessible sexual role for their own purposes, whatever these might be. An example of this troubling discourse occurred in *Evans*, where the undercover operatives were dealing with a target of sub-normal intelligence who had extensive brain damage from being run down by a truck when he was nine years of age (para. 1). Mr. Justice Preston described the undercover officers' comments to Evans: "one of the officers, [UC1], indicated that he needed to teach 'a bitch' a lesson and needed someplace to dispose of the body. Fellow undercover officers later told Mr. Evans that UC1 had killed a fourteen year old girl 'after screwing her'" (1996, para. 13). After Evans denied having "screwed young girls," two officers "discussed how tight young girls were" (para. 17). The victims in the homicide investigation were two adult women.

As they did in other cases, the undercover officers "typically spent their time [with Evans] drinking and watching strippers, discussing sexual exploits in the grossest possible language" (para. 7). Wade Skiffington, another target, reports similar terminology used by the undercover operators: "Bitch, go put on some clothes. You fucking whore" (Maidment 2009: 99). Maidment describes this "hyper-masculinity" and other tactics (such as the use of drugs, alcohol and illegal activities) of the undercover operators as "nothing short of offensive and shocking" (2009: 104).

Undercover Mr. Big operatives claim that people who stand in their way can be terminated, and in a number of cases they have simulated killings and severe beatings. Here is newspaper coverage of the Mr. Big operation against Wade Skiffington:

> Set inside a moving car, the scene involved a pregnant woman, and a man said to have stolen $300,000, from the boss…. Almost immediately, the two men started fighting… the woman pleading for the beating to stop, the man in front screaming in pain… the man and woman were forced out of the car into the snow… the [undercover operators] put a gun to the back of the kneeling man's head… threaten[ed] to kill them both…. "The woman gets it

first through the gut. I'll kill the baby first." (quoted in Gorbet 2004: 55; see also Maidment 2009: 96–97)

According to Mr. Justice Preston in *Evans*, "The climate created by the undercover operators was a climate of lawlessness and killing in which they did what they wanted to their great financial profit and were protected by the resources of the 'organization'" (para. 15). As pointed out above, in some cases the undercover officers actually break the law (without authorization under section 25.1 of the *Criminal Code*) and counsel their targets to do likewise. In some cases, even the judges excuse this illegal activity as part of the prop in the undercover operation.

At other times, undercover officers may suggest killing someone for no apparent reason. In *Doyle*, an undercover officer pretended he was looking for someone to "whack his old lady." Doyle said he could arrange the killing so that someone else would be blamed for it (2003: para. 45). In *Hathway*, the undercover officers simulated the beating of a woman and threw her in the trunk of a car. During the beating, "the major operative threatened to kill the woman, her spousal partner, and their two-year old child." Hathway feared for his own safety and that of his child (2007: para. 19).

Studies on police deviance and corruption suggest that police deviance is rooted in group behaviour and work context (Punch 2000; Porter 2009). If this is the case, when police officers role-play criminals to solve difficult homicide cases, the perfect scenario is created for "noble cause" corruption (also referred to as the "Dirty Harry syndrome") (Punch 2000: 305). Noble cause corruption "involves using illicit means for organizationally and socially approved ends" (305). It often takes place in results-oriented, specialized police units (312), and involves bending the rules and the evidence to get a conviction against someone the police officers believe is guilty. The pressure in a Mr. Big operation, from the public and internally, is to resolve a murder case. Operatives become very focussed on this goal.

Noble cause corruption can lead police officers to refuse to accept reality or to accept the fact that due process means that some individuals they believe to be guilty will be found not guilty. They refuse to accept that "there are no unjust acquittals" (Sorochan 2008: 438) in our due process system. The Mr. Big investigation against Hennessey and Cheeseman appears to be an example of the police inability to accept the reality that four of their fellow officers died at the hands of one man (Roszko). The parole officer who interviewed Hennessey and Cheeseman after their guilty pleas believed the two men were "victims of both Roszko and of a misguided RCMP 'witch hunt' to blame someone for the crimes of Roszko and for the RCMP's own mishandling of the matter" (Staples 2010).

Mr. Big scenarios are also conducive to group think. According to Porter, "Group think is particularly likely under conditions of high stress, where groups believe in their own morality, feel a unanimity or high cohesiveness and where there is an absence of external audit" (2009: 95). Since much of the grooming of the target is typically done without surveillance, there is opportunity to bend the rules. Noble cause corruption and group think can lead to wrongful convictions — an issue we return to in the final chapter.

The moral issues in Mr. Big operations raise a number of questions. If, as Leo, suggests, police interrogations "go to the heart of our conceptions of procedural fairness and substantive justice and raise questions about the kind of criminal justice system and society we wish to have" (2008: 1), do we want police officers to engage in derogatory activities in order to investigate crimes? Do we want them to use public funds to engage in these activities? What effect does role-playing actually have on the psyche of the undercover officers, their targets, and others within hearing and viewing distance? Is the price paid for a confession worth the cost? Do these tactics violate fundamentals freedoms we expect to find in a free and democratic society? Are there ways to reign in the Mr. Big investigative technique and make it workable, or should it be condemned as it was in 1901, as "vile," "base," and "contemptible" (*Todd*: paras. 3 and 8)?

Notes

1. Moore, Copeland, and Schuller (2009: 360) suggest that this could be done without jeopardizing undercover operations designed to investigate ongoing criminal activities. In addition, the entrapment laws (which don't apply to Mr. Big investigations) put some limits on what undercover officers can do when investigating ongoing activities.
2. Although counsel for the accused in *Roop* (2007) was able to convince the trial judge that the accused knew that the undercover police officers were police officers, the judge, in any event, ruled that Roop's confession was voluntary.
3. Examples of police trickery that may shock the community were set out in *Rothman* (1981) and later affirmed in *Oickle* (2000), and include "a police officer pretending to be a chaplain or a legal aid lawyer, or injecting truth serum into a diabetic under the pretense that it was insulin" (para. 66).
4. British Columbia Court of Appeal decisions: *Bonisteel* (2008); *Fischer* (2005a); *Forknall* (2003a); *French* (1997); *McCreery* (1998a); *Skiffington* (2004); *Terrico* (2005a); Ontario Court of Appeal decision: *Osmar* (2007a).
5. Dr. Lohrasbe did not give evidence as to whether the accused confessed falsely, but "was called to testify only as to the nature of a false confession, and to confirm that they do exist" (*C.K.R.S.* 2005: para. 89).
6. See Anderson and Anderson's (2009: 16–20) discussion of how the marginalized and underprivileged, those who live on the fringes of society, are overrepresented in the criminal justice system.
7. Griffin, an alcoholic, testified that he was drinking excessively during the undercover operation, and the trial judge found that he was impaired during some of the meetings with the undercover officer (paras. 43–44). He was also paid substantial amounts of money for the work he did and was told that the "sky was the limit" in terms of the money he could make (para. 45).
8. This book is not suggesting that suspects in the other cases did not disclose details withheld from publication, only that it was not discussed in the available data sources.
9. In *Dix* (2001), Sergeant Greg Smith, NCO in charge of Undercover Coordination for

the "K" Division of the RCMP (Edmonton, Alberta), testified that several undercover operations had to be terminated because officer safety was compromised (paras. 15–19).

10. Sections 666 and 360 of the *Criminal Code* also provide exceptions to the general rule. See Brockman and Rose 2011: 281–82; *B. (F.F.)* 1993: para. 72; *G. (S.G.)* 1997: para. 63; *B. (C.R.)* 1990: at 744.

5

Reining In Mr. Big

This study set out to provide a better understanding of the nature and scope of a controversial undercover investigative technique widely known as Mr. Big. An analysis of the means used to groom contacts and elicit confessions from them, and of eighty-one judicial decisions involving the Mr. Big technique over the past seventeen years, clearly demonstrates that, despite the successes of this technique, serious questions remain about the reliability of some of these confessions and the impact that the technique has on due process considerations integral to our criminal justice system.

Law enforcement officers claim that the Mr. Big investigative technique provides them with a last-resort tool to gather otherwise unavailable information about a criminal event and suspect, to secure crucial evidence, and, in most cases, to obtain a conviction in serious criminal investigations that have reached an impasse (*Hathway* 2007: para. 8; see also Motto and June 2000: 2). Some investigative files can lie dormant for extended periods of time; were it not for the Mr. Big technique, officers argue, these crimes would almost certainly remain unsolved, shelved indefinitely as cold case files (*Black* 2006: para. 77; *Cretney* 1999: para. 4; *Ethier* 2004: paras. 8–10; *Simmonds* 2000a: para. 6; *Skiffington* 2004: para. 8; *Unger* 1993b: para. 80).

The case of Gregory Parsons is illustrative. On February 15, 1994, following a trial by judge and jury, Parsons was found guilty of the second-degree murder of his mother, Catherine Ann Carroll, and was subsequently sentenced to life imprisonment with no eligibility for parole for fifteen years (*Parsons* 1996: para. 1). Mr. Justice O'Neill, for the Newfoundland Court of Appeal, observed that there was no direct evidence implicating Gregory Parsons in the death of his mother; the Crown's case was circumstantial (para. 40). In addition, the court found that the prejudicial effect of other pieces of evidence substantially outweighed any probative value they might have had. Mr. Justice O'Neill ruled, "the errors of law which I have found here are serious ones and I cannot conclude that the verdict would necessarily have been the same if these errors had not occurred" (para. 68). Parsons' conviction was quashed on appeal, and the Newfoundland Court of Appeal ordered a new trial (para. 71). However, advancements in DNA analysis allowed the crime laboratory in Ottawa to conclude that "the male DNA found on the submitted items was not that of Gregory Parsons" (Government of Newfoundland and Labrador 1998). As a result, the Crown entered a stay of proceedings in the case. While Parsons received an apology from both the Minister of Justice and the Attorney General and was offered compensation (*Doyle* 2003: para. 2), his mother's killer remained at large.

The newly acquired DNA evidence enabled the police to renew a more broadly focused investigation. The Royal Newfoundland Constabulary set its sights on Brian Doyle, targeting him in a Mr. Big undercover operation. During this investigation, Doyle identified the site where the murder weapon could be found. The result of all of this, according to Chief Justice Green of the trial division of the Newfoundland and Labrador Supreme Court, was that twelve years after death, the question of who killed Catherine Carroll could finally be answered (*Doyle* 2003: para. 5).

Despite apparent successes of this kind and of claims that the overall success rate is high, serious questions remain about the methods and the impact of the Mr. Big investigative technique. The RCMP (2009) claims that "Charges are always supported with corroborating physical evidence and/or compelling circumstantial evidence, in addition to any admission that may have been obtained through the undercover operation." Yet we found twenty-three cases where the accused's self-incriminating statements to undercover police officers were essential to the prosecution's case. Without these statements, there would have been no basis for a conviction (see *Bridges* 2005a: para. 19; *Ciancio* 2006: para. 162; *C.K.R.S.* 2005: para. 75; *Fischer* 2005: para. 55; *Fliss* 2002: para. 20; *Forknall* 2000: para. 8; *Griffin* 2001a: para. 62; *G.W.F.* 2003a: para. 11; *Hambleton* 2006: para. 8; *Hennessey* 2008; *Lowe* 2009: para. 23; *McCreery* 1998: para. 12; *Osmar* 2007a: para. 2; *Peterffy* 2000: para. 9; *Proulx* 2005; *R.K.C.* 2004: para. 16; *Roberts* 1997: para. 15; *Simmonds* 2000b: para. 6; *Skiffington* 2004: para. 11; *Smith* 2003: para. 12; *T.C.M.* 2007: para. 19; *Valliere* 2004: paras. 33 and 38; and see Joyce 2008 for Fry). As we point out in our discussion of the *Unger* case (later in this chapter), sometimes other supporting evidence, which subsequently proves to be inaccurate, can be more readily ignored when the accused has "confessed."

Questions arise about the reliability of these confessions. Although confessions obtained through a Mr. Big operation might not be the result of direct threats or outright violence, undercover operatives do cultivate an atmosphere of fear and intimidation to convey a convincing image of corruption, and consequently targets may confess out of fear of reprisal. Also, statements are invariably induced by promises of wealth and professional advancement in a sophisticated criminal organization, not to mention the prospect of avoiding criminal sanctions by having the organization help conceal a crime. Despite safeguards that, according to the RCMP, "ensure" assertions obtained from targets are trustworthy, these incidents undermine the reliability of self-incriminating statements by increasing the chances that an innocent person might confess to a crime he or she did not commit. Conceivably, a conviction can be sustained on the basis of confession evidence alone, even when the validity of the confession is brought into question.

As was discussed in Chapter 2, confession evidence has been shown to have a significant biasing effect on the perceptions and decision-making process of jurors (Conti 1999; Driver, 1968; Drizin and Leo 2004; Kassin and Sukel 1997; Kassin and Neumann 1997; Kassin and Wrightsman 1980, 1981; Leo and Ofshe 1998a; Wrightsman, Nietzel, and Fortune 1994). As Wrightsman (1991) points out, "It seems that what you say is more influential than why you say it" (170). All things considered, confession evidence is often seen as incontrovertible evidence of guilt. Accordingly, it is essential that the Canadian criminal justice system have in place measures to minimize the risk that innocent people will confess to, and subsequently be convicted of, crimes they did not commit.

"Setting Public Policy on the Parameters of Undercover Operations" [1]

Conceptually, the Mr. Big investigative technique is creatively fashioned to obtain incriminating evidence in the form of a confession from a suspect in a serious criminal investigation that has reached an impasse, and it is designed with built-in safeguards to avoid eliciting unreliable, misleading, and/or erroneous information from unwitting suspects. As this analysis has shown, however, the potential for false confessions also exists. Although modern psychological interrogation techniques are designed to secure incriminating information from allegedly guilty suspects, interrogators are equally capable of eliciting confessions from innocent persons (Kassin 1997: 221). Ofshe and Leo (1997b) point out that modern interrogation tactics, "if misdirected, used ineptly, or utilized improperly, sometimes convince ordinary, psychologically and intellectually normal individuals to falsely confess" (984). To prevent the elicitation of erroneous confessions and the miscarriages of justice that might ensue, Drizin and Leo (2004) recommend greater education and training of law enforcement personnel about the causes, indicators, and consequences of false confessions (997–1003).

This chapter examines seven recommendations for legal reforms to the Mr. Big operation that could help prevent the elicitation of false confessions and further miscarriages of justice in the Canadian criminal justice system: 1) requiring the police to obtain prior judicial authorization to conduct a Mr. Big operation; 2) treating self-incriminating statements obtained in Mr. Big operations as hearsay that requires necessity and reliability as preconditions to its admissibility; 3) requiring corroboration for statements made in a Mr. Big investigation; 4) requiring that jurors be warned of the possibility of false admissions; 5) using expert evidence to assist the trier of fact; 6) extending the right to silence, as protected by section 7 of the *Canadian Charter of Rights and Freedoms*, to this undercover technique; and 7) treating undercover police officers as persons in authority and therefore requiring that admissions be voluntary. Lastly, we examine the option of adopting a general exclusionary rule with respect to confessions obtained through Mr. Big undercover operations in order to avoid false confessions and maintain the integrity of the criminal justice system.

Obtaining Prior Judicial Authorization

The data in this study illustrate that undercover police officers, posing as members of a sophisticated criminal organization in their endeavour to ascertain whether a suspect is criminally responsible, employ interrogation tactics that call into question the voluntariness of, and undermine the reliability of, assertions made by the suspect. Some legal commentators have proposed that prior judicial authorization be required as a means of scrutinizing and limiting these undercover operations. Penney (2004), for example, writes,

> If we were truly concerned about protecting suspects from unwarranted invasions of privacy and betrayals of trust, then police would be required to obtain prior authorization for all undercover elicitation attempts (whether before or after detention), just as we do for electronic surveillance. (328)

Presently, police officers obtain prior judicial authorization either under section 184.2 of the *Criminal Code* to intercept communications by consent of one of the parties (usually Mr. Big or a police informant) or under section 186 to intercept private communications without the consent of either party. Obviously, if the police are concerned with only the discussions between their operatives and the target, section 184.2 authorization is sufficient and the police need to establish only that there is consent by the undercover operatives and reasonable grounds to believe that information concerning an offence will be obtained. Without the one-party consent, the police will need to undergo the more onerous task of applying for authorization under section 186, which requires police officers to establish:

> (a) that it would be in the best interests of the administration of justice to do so; and
> (b) that other investigative procedures have been tried and have failed, other investigative procedures are unlikely to succeed or the urgency of the matter is such that it would be impractical to carry out the investigation of the offence using only other investigative procedures.[2]

In this study, authorization for consent surveillance (i.e., section 184.2) was mentioned in ten cases and authorization for surveillance without consent (i.e., section 186) was mentioned in thirteen cases.[3] Given the importance of recording confessions to Mr. Big, one might assume that the police apply for one or the other type of authorization in most scenarios and that they disclose aspects of their Mr. Big plans to the authorizing judge. This appeared obvious, for instance, in the ruling by Chief Justice Hewak of the Manitoba Court of Queen's Bench concerning the admissibility of intercepted conversations between the accused and undercover officers in *Unger* (1992):

The undercover operation occurred in circumstances of necessity. Clearly other normal investigative procedures had been tried, but had not succeeded, and in the opinion of the investigating police officers were unlikely to succeed. They felt that if the accused Unger had been approached by police officers in any direct fashion, based on his previous reaction to them, they would have been unsuccessful in receiving any useful or additional information from him. There was no other method by which this information could be obtained. (para. 15)

Unquestionably, the crime with which we are concerned, is a particularly brutal killing of a young girl. That killing would have been left unsolved without the kind of information that the undercover police were able to obtain from the accused Unger. (para. 17)

Be that as it may, since the police are seeking approval to intercept conversations and not to engage in a Mr. Big scenario, it is doubtful that the evidence disclosed in the officers' affidavits filed in support of the request for an authorization outlined their undercover methodology and operational plans or that the judge scrutinized the Mr. Big operation for the possibility of producing unreliable evidence. There is even less scrutiny required to obtain authorization for consent surveillance under section 184.2. As noted by Mr. Justice Romilly in *McCreery* (1996), "the requirements for obtaining the authorization under the consent provision are not as stringent under s. 184.2 as those under s. 186" because officers need not demonstrate investigative necessity (para. 38).[4] Furthermore, a Mr. Big operation can conceivably commence without the interception of private communication and therefore without any prior judicial authorization for electronic surveillance.

Should the police be required to obtain authorization for a Mr. Big scenario, and give a detailed explanation of their operational plans before commencing their investigation? As a matter of policy, would it be possible under such authorizations to establish procedural parameters limiting the type and size of inducements police officers hold out to targets, as well as restricting violence, intimidation, psychological manipulation, and implied threats of physical harm utilized to convey a convincingly corrupt image?

While the overall undercover operation has a central theme, and some scenarios may be scripted and planned, most of the meetings are developed as a result of the target's reaction to scenarios previously played out (*Hart* 2007: para. 19). That is to say, officers may have but a moment's notice to engage a suspect in a scenario, thus requiring police to improvise as the operation unfolds. Testifying before a superior court judge in Québec, RCMP officer Serge Coulombe said, "It's like writing a book, with chapters that follow one another" (Cherry 2005: A8). Another undercover operative stated, "Everything is based on day-to-day situations and how the target reacts to what happened that day" (Baron 2008b: A8).

While there is some merit to the suggestion that the police receive prior authorization before conducting a Mr. Big operation, numerous complications could arise. As alluded to earlier, only a handful of investigators are made aware of the holdback evidence in an investigation. This tactical decision helps to prevent contamination and preserve the integrity and trustworthiness of suspects' assertions. Compelling the police to disclose particulars in their affidavits increases the number of people privy to these details, thus increasing the possibility of contamination. Furthermore, once the range of tactics police officers are able to employ is limited, the task of conveying the impression that they are hardened and ruthless criminals becomes difficult. These kinds of strictures not only run the risk of compromising the investigation, but also, more importantly, undermine the safety of undercover officers.

Though open to conjecture, the argument could be made that the three techniques to enhance the reliability of disclosures discussed in Chapter Four (i.e., the adherence to the code of trust, honesty, and loyalty; contamination of holdback evidence; and clandestine audio and video recording), in combination with proper education and training of law enforcement personnel about the "causes, indicia, and consequences of false confessions," would theoretically work to prevent the elicitation of false confessions (Drizin and Leo 2004: 997). Perhaps more useful would be a more thorough screening of the alleged confessions at the trial stage.

A Principled Approach Requirement of Necessity and Reliability

As stated earlier in this book, whether an out-of-court statement made by an accused person to an undercover police officer is regarded as an exception to the hearsay rule requiring the Crown to prove necessity and reliability is an issue that has yet to be resolved by Canada's highest court. However, the majority of decisions on Mr. Big operations have been in favour of not requiring necessity and reliability as prerequisites to admitting statements during Mr. Big operations at the subsequent trials of the accused.

The admissions exception to the hearsay rule rests on the assumption that, because people do not commonly make statements against their own interest unless they are true, admissions against interest are sufficiently reliable to be admitted as substantive evidence (Brockman and Rose 2011: 219). The quandary that arises with regard to this proposition is that a target's confession to undercover police officers posing as criminals is "not against interest since the suspect believes that it is in his interest to admit to a crime to fellow criminals" (*Osmar* 2007a: para. 52). For that reason, the courts or Parliament should consider changing the law so that admissions made during Mr. Big scenarios are exceptions to the hearsay rule requiring necessity and reliability as preconditions to their admissibility.

There were no arguments put forward on the issue of necessity in any of the ten cases where the accused argued that his or her admissions to undercover police officers were hearsay requiring the application of necessity and reliability analysis of the principled exception to the hearsay rule. In some cases, the accused conceded that the requirement of necessity was met (see *Unger* 2005a: para. 9).

One of the evidentiary dangers normally associated with the admission of hearsay evidence is the "inability of the trier of fact to assess the demeanour of the declarant" (*Hawkins* 1996, para: 67). One approach that could alleviate such concerns is to require the mandatory videotaping of all undercover elicitation attempts, thus giving the trier of fact the opportunity to assess the demeanour of the accused. However, the grooming of targets can take many months and involve up to fifty operatives (Moore, Copeland, and Schuller 2009: 349), and videotaping or even recording these activities may not be practical. As explained by Mr. Justice Menzies in *Bridges* (2005), "The statements of the accused can only be obtained through his mouth and as he is not a compellable witness in his own trial, the statements given to the undercover police officer are the only other source of this evidence" (para. 13).

Concerning the criterion of reliability, the role of the trial judge is limited to ascertaining whether the hearsay statement "exhibits sufficient indicia of reliability so as to afford the trier of fact a satisfactory basis for evaluating the truth of the statement" (*Hawkins* 1996: para. 75). The ultimate reliability or truth of the hearsay statement, and the weight to be attached to it, remain determinations for the trier of fact (para. 75) — in most of these cases, a jury.

Both the Alberta Court of Appeal in *Wytyshyn* (2002: para. 7–8), and the Manitoba Court of Queen's Bench in *Bridges* (2005a, 2005b) applied the reliability analysis of the principled exception to the hearsay rule, and both courts ruled that the accused's statements to undercover police officers met the threshold test of reliability. The ultimate test of reliability is left to the trier of fact. Even in cases where the judiciary ruled that the accused's confessions were an exception to the hearsay rule, those statements were held to be admissible because the evidence, in any event, supported a finding of threshold reliability (*Perovic* 2004a: paras. 21–23). With the exception of extraordinary circumstances, it appears as though the judiciary will invariably rule the accused's confession to Mr. Big meets the required degree of threshold reliability.

Taking into account the circumstances in which a statement is obtained, is a threshold test for reliability sufficient? Would it be dangerous to accept an accused person's confession as reliable without confirmation from some other independent source?

Requiring Corroboration

That confession evidence is often unreliable and the basis for miscarriages of justice is no longer conjecture; it is a reality supported by the literature on the general phenomenon of false confessions (Gohara 2005: 837). Gohara (2006) suggests that "no criminal prosecution should proceed on the basis of the defendant's uncorroborated self-incriminating statement alone" (837; also see Sangero 2007). Statements obtained as a result of a Mr. Big sting should be *prima facie* inadmissible as evidence *unless* there is confirmation by other independent, reliable evidence.

Drizin and Leo (2004) suggest that, initially, a confession "should be treated as a neutral hypothesis to be objectively tested against the case facts" (999). If the suspect gives a comprehensive narrative that is consistent with the facts of the case, or discloses information that was unknown to police or is corroborated by other independent, reliable evidence, such as a guilty knowledge of the crime (e.g., leading police to missing evidence, giving details that only the perpetrator would know), then the confession demonstrates an indicia of reliability and high probative value (Gudjonsson 1992: 259; Leo and Ofshe 1998a: 439; Osmar 2007a: para. 62). Conversely, if the suspect does not possess actual knowledge of the crime, is unable to provide accurate information not already known to the police, or gives demonstrably incorrect details about the crime scene, then the statement should be considered unreliable and have no evidentiary value (Leo and Ofshe 1998a: 439). In addition, Leo and Ofshe (1998a) posit that it is the mundane details related to the criminal event that are of great worth in determining guilt or innocence because mundane facts are "less likely to be the result of contamination by the police" (440).

As an alternative method, Ofshe and Leo (1997b; Leo and Ofshe 1998a) contend that the reliability of a confession can be evaluated by answering at least three questions: (1) Does the suspect's statement lead to the discovery of evidence that was previously unknown to the police (e.g., a location of a missing murder weapon or a body)? (2) Does the statement include highly unusual features of the crime that have been held back from the public (e.g., details of how the body was discovered, the cause of death)? (3) Does the suspect provide accurate descriptions of the mundane details pertaining to the crime scene that have not been made public (e.g., the type of clothing the victim was wearing)? (cited in Gudjonsson 2003b: 179). It should, however, be noted that suspects can provide information on all of these criteria without being the person who committed the crime.

Mandatory Warnings to Jurors

If Mr. Big confessions are ruled admissible, they should be followed by mandatory instructions to the jury about the inherent unreliability of a confession made in these non-custodial circumstances. A priority for the criminal courts should be a "specific formulation" of a Hodgson-type warning, as it relates to the reliability of the statements made by the accused to undercover police officers, that goes beyond advising the trier of fact that "a confession obtained under oppressive or fearful circumstances may not be reliable and must be scrutinized with care" (Carter 2001: para. 59). Though well intentioned, this advice does little to enlighten laypeople about the elements of modern psychological interrogation (particularly the processes involved in the Mr. Big strategy) that result in false confessions, and does little to counterbalance the psychological myth of interrogation, that innocent people rarely confess to crimes that they did not commit (Dufraimont 2008: para. 13).

Although a confession obtained through a Mr. Big undercover operation might not be the result of direct threats or outright violence, the opportunity structure (e.g., financial inducements, professional advancement, and intoxication), coupled with an atmosphere of fear and intimidation, could increase the likelihood that an innocent person confesses to a crime. More needs to be done to sensitize jurors about the frailties of confessions made in undercover operations like the Mr. Big strategy. Dufraimont (2008) argues that a cautionary instruction ought to "convey the necessary education about unreliable confessions, while remaining as unambiguous and protracted as possible" (para. 59). Mr. Justice Williams' forthright statement in *Perovic* would be an appropriate foundation. Both the content and language of this prospective instruction are not so overly esoteric as to confuse the trier of fact:

> I recognize that such undercover operations tend to encourage false bravado and boastfulness in the targets. There is a real concern that the targets will exaggerate their role in any activity. I am aware that the statements thus made are not contrary to the penal interest of the subject but, rather, occur in an atmosphere where there is a pressure upon the subject to claim credit for criminal activity. I recognize that the undercover operators often make generous payments to targets for their performance of apparent criminal activities, that they hold out a powerful inducement of membership in a sophisticated and wealthy organization, and that the target engages in dealings with individuals who are made to appear powerful and capable of great violence. (2004b, para. 25)

Some commentators have indicated that confession evidence influences not only the perceptions and decision-making of lay jurors, but also of criminal justice officials (i.e., judges) (Kassin and Sukel 1997: 42–44; Leo 1996a: 301; Leo 2007: 31; Leo 2009; Leo and Ofshe 1998a: 478). Penney (2004), for instance, suggests that some judges might not be sufficiently conscious of, or are ill-informed about, the phenomenon of false confessions (296). Thus, in circumstances where the accused elects a trial by superior court judge alone, it is imperative that the warnings extend to the judiciary as well. This is especially important in cases involving confessions obtained by virtue of a Mr. Big operation because sixteen of the eighty-one cases were tried before a superior court judge alone.

The Use of Expert Opinion Evidence to Assist the Trier of Fact

Although opinion evidence is generally prohibited at trial, there is an established exception to the rule that permits an expert to give opinion evidence if it is necessary to assist the trier of fact on an issue outside their experience or knowledge (Brockman and Rose 2011: 304). In other words, it must be relevant to a fact in issue. In *Mohan* (1994), Mr. Justice Sopinka clarified the circumstances in which expert evidence is admissible as evidence. The trial judge, he stated, must be satisfied that the witness has the appropriate expertise based four criteria: relevance, necessity in assisting the trier of fact, the absence of any exclusionary rule, and proper qualifications (para. 17).

With these criteria in mind, one might ask, is the Mr. Big scenario a matter for which expert evidence is required?

At Timothy Osmar's trial, counsel for the accused sought to call Dr. Richard Ofshe to testify about the reasons why suspects might falsely confess and about the proper method for evaluating the reliability of a confession. On a *voir dire*, Dr. Ofshe explained that,

> where the reasons not to confess are sufficiently reduced by making the suspect believe that resistance is hopeless and that some advantage may come from confession, both the likelihood of confession and the risk of false confession will rise. It may eventually become attractive to a suspect to admit a crime. (*Osmar* 2007a: para. 20)

In addition, he testified that, indeed, the notion that people would not confess to a crime they did not commit is still very much prevalent among laypeople and criminal justice officials. Dr. Ofshe's role as an expert would be "to try to dispel certain myths that are widely held, and also to make clear a simple analytic structure for understanding this particular interrogation strategy" (para. 62). Lastly, it was Dr. Ofshe's opinion that Osmar's confession to undercover police officers was contaminated with information relayed to Osmar by investigating officers who interrogated him prior to the undercover operation (para. 21). These opinions helped to delineate the process for evaluating the veracity of a confession.

Dr. Ofshe conceded that he had not studied the Mr. Big strategy *per se*, "but believed that his analysis of statements to known persons in authority could be adapted to the Mr. Big method" (para. 20). Since Dr. Ofshe was proposing to apply his expertise in custodial interrogations to the Mr. Big strategy, the trial judge was of the view that he was advancing a novel scientific theory and should therefore be subject to special scrutiny to determine whether it met a specific threshold (para. 63).[5] Having applied the test for the admission of expert evidence set out *Mohan* (1994) and *J.-L.J.* (2000), the trial judge held that Dr. Ofshe's evidence "did not meet the requirements of relevancy and necessity for admission of expert evidence" (*Osmar* 2007a: paras. 63–64). The Ontario Court of Appeal affirmed the trial judge's ruling. Justice Rosenberg, for the Court, held that Dr. Ofshe's evidence "was not about matters on which ordinary people are unlikely to form a correct judgment" (para. 68). Leave to appeal to the Supreme Court of Canada was refused (2007).

The British Columbia Court of Appeal in *Bonisteel* (2008) was asked to decide whether the trial judge erred by not allowing the accused to call a psychologist to give expert opinion evidence on false confessions (para. 25). As in the *Osmar* case, the expert witness was not familiar with the specific undercover operation in issue.

Moreover, the psychologist's evidence was based not on a clinical evaluation or interviews, but on a review of the relevant literature (para. 62). Citing the test for the admissibility of expert evidence established in *Mohan* (1994), the trial judge ruled that the psychologist's evidence was inadmissible because it was neither relevant nor necessary to assist the trier of fact. On appeal, Mme. Justice Levine saw no reason to interfere with the trial judge's ruling, finding that the proposed evidence "did not deal with the specific nature of the evidence in this case, but only with matters about which the jury could form a judgment based on their own experience, assisted by instructions from the trial judge" (para. 69).

Given the fact that scientific understanding of the phenomenon of false confessions is still in its formative years, the debate as to whether this body of literature has "reached a sufficient level of maturity for the purposes of expert testimony" continues (Trotter 2004: para. 32). The courts here in Canada have ruled expert evidence related to the phenomenon of false confessions inadmissible, and it remains categorized as a novel science (Dufraimont 2008; Trotter 2004). As evidenced in the two preceding cases, advancing a theory that proposes to explain the counterintuitive myth of psychological interrogation, that innocent people sometimes confess to crimes that they did not commit, has been rejected by the courts as not "likely to be outside the experience and knowledge of a judge or jury" (*Mohan* 1994: para. 22). While commentators in this area agree that this knowledge can be conveyed to the jury via judicial instruction, they posit that jurors are unlikely to understand *how* and *why* the phenomenon of false confessions occurs (Dufraimont 2008; Trotter 2004).

The conduct of an accused person during an interrogation, especially when subjected to modern psychological interrogation techniques, is not within the normal experience of jurors. It is the role of the jury to determine the ultimate reliability of an out-of-court statement and the weight to be attached to it. Given the Supreme Court of Canada's recognition in *Oickle* (2000) that false confessions stem from exceptional techniques or strategies employed by the police during interrogation, expert evidence related to these specific techniques, and how they undermine the reliability of confessions obtained from them, would be of great assistance to a jury in determining the truth or falsehood of assertions made by an accused person (see Trotter 2004: para. 27).

While the admissibility of expert psychological testimony in relation to disputed confessions has been rejected by Canadian criminal courts, Gudjonsson (2003a) points out that in the United Kingdom, the expert opinion of clinical psychologists has had a profound effect on the practice and ruling of the Court of Appeal in England and Wales, as well as the British House of Lords (159). He reviewed twenty-two high-profile murder cases in England and Wales where convictions based on confession evidence were overturned on appeal between 1989 and 2001 (Gudjonsson 2003a: 165). In eleven of the twenty-two cases, Gudjonsson found the psychological evidence to be most influential on appeal.

As Gudjonsson's (2003a) interactional model for assessing the outcome of police interviews illustrates, there are numerous potential factors that make some individuals more susceptible to the pressures of modern psychological interrogation. The underlying message from his analysis is that "each case must be considered on its own merit" (165). Within his sample of cases, a recurring issue that led to the suspect's giving false confessions was the inability of the suspect to cope with the pressures of custody and police questioning (165). This analysis, although modest, confirms the notion that false confessions can be elicited from cognitively and intellectually normal individuals (Leo and Ofshe 1998a; Drizin and Leo 2004, Gudjonsson 2003b).

The next recommendation advocates extending an accused's constitutional right to silence as protected by the common law and section 7 of the *Canadian Charter of Rights and Freedoms.*

The Common Law and Constitutional Right to Silence

As discussed in Chapter 4, the right to silence, according to the Supreme Court of Canada, does not extend to protecting suspects against police tricks during the pre-detention period (*Turcotte* 2005: para. 51).[6] Accordingly, the Courts have invariably ruled that undercover operatives who engage suspects in a Mr. Big scenario do not have control over an individual's movements so as to deprive the suspect of their constitutional right to silence. The undercover operation takes place during the investigative stage, and suspects are not being detained for investigative purposes or placed under arrest at the material time statements are made to undercover officers.

Returning to the Supreme Court of Canada's decision in *Hebert* (1990), Justices Wilson and Sopinka dissented from the majority decision, expressing the view that the right to silence "must arise whenever the coercive power of the state is brought to bear upon the citizen.... [T]his could well predate detention and extend to the police interrogation of a suspect" (para. 94).

It is easy to see how this distinction can be blurred, so that suspects who make self-incriminating statements to undercover operators are, in certain circumstances, theoretically deprived of a "free and meaningful choice as to whether to speak to the authorities or to remain silent" (*Hebert* 1990: para. 67). In *McIntyre* (1993), Mr. Justice Rice was heedful of the fact that at the time of his arrest and detention, and after consulting with legal counsel, McIntyre informed the police of his choice to remain silent (para. 12). Notwithstanding this choice, the police placed a "cell plant" in McIntyre's cell in order to initiate contact with and introduce him to an undercover operative purporting to be a criminal and ex-convict. Upon his release from custody, this criminal figure was able to locate McIntyre in the community and, after some time, elicit self-incriminating statements from him. As Mr. Justice Rice observed in his dissenting opinion, the "cell plant" operation undertaken by undercover operatives had its "beginnings during detention" and "successfully continued afterward" (para. 15). While the Supreme Court of Canada dismissed

McIntyre's appeal on this issue, it did so in oral reasons without a full analysis.

It is time for the Courts to consider extending the scope of an accused person's constitutional right to silence to suspects targeted in Mr. Big operations, particularly in circumstances where undercover operatives initiate contact with their target while he or she is in police custody (e.g., by placing an undercover operator posing as a criminal in a police transport vehicle or in a holding cell with the suspect). Perhaps the right to remain silent should extend to all Mr. Big operations. This would mean that undercover officers would not be allowed to elicit statements from targets (*Hebert* 1990; *Liew* 1999).

If an accused person's constitutional right to silence is violated during a Mr. Big operation by an agent of the state, he or she may seek a remedy under section 24(2) of the *Charter*. The Supreme Court of Canada has recently replaced the *Collins/Stillman* test with the *Grant* framework (*Grant* 2009) for determining whether evidence obtained in violation of one's *Charter* rights would bring the administration of justice into disrepute. To assess whether to exclude evidence the section 24(2) analysis now includes the following three components: "1) the seriousness of the *Charter*-infringing state conduct; 2) the impact of the breach on the *Charter*-protected interests of the accused; and 3) society's interest in the adjudication of the case on its merits" (para. 71 and 85).

If the right to remain silent were extended to all pre-detention circumstances, the ramifications would prohibit undercover police officers from actively eliciting information from suspects who are not detained. Without the ability to actively elicit statements from a suspect during the Mr. Big interrogatory ruse, would the police be able to feasibly conduct a Mr. Big scenario? In theory, yes, but it would take much longer to conduct an undercover investigation. Would this change bring about the disintegration and downfall of the Mr. Big investigative strategy?

Modifying the Common Law Confessions Rule

The common law confessions rule, which requires the Crown to prove that statements made by an accused to a person in authority were made voluntarily, is ostensibly to safeguard against false confessions (*Oickle* 2000: para 32). However, as Trotter notes (2004: para. 14), the voluntariness, not the truthfulness, of a confession is the focus of the *voir dire* to decide its admissibility. The truthfulness is an issue left to the fact trier. Even so, if the interrogation techniques or strategies employed by the police (in this case, undercover police officers who are not considered persons in authority) do not fall within the ambit of the rule, how then can admissions to Mr. Big be monitored so as to reduce the possibility of false confessions and resulting miscarriages of justice?

In *Oickle* (2000), the Supreme Court of Canada remarked, "Voluntariness is the touchstone of the confessions rule" (para. 69).[7] This underlying principle is based on the notion that "involuntary confessions are more likely to be unreliable" (para. 32). A confession induced by a "fear of prejudice" or "hope of advantage" held out by persons in authority (persons who the accused believes are able to affect the course of the prosecution) is not only involuntary but is likely to have little indicia of reliability, and is generally inadmissible as evidence against an accused (*Ibrahim v. The King* 1914: 609; *Oickle* 2000: para. 15). Significantly, as stated earlier in this book, the requirement that admissions be voluntary applies only to statements made to persons in authority. Consequently, self-incriminating statements gleaned from unwitting suspects by undercover police officers who portray themselves as members of a criminal organization do not fall within the ambit of the common law confessions rule.

Mr. Justice De Villiers of the B.C. Provincial Court in *Copeland* (1995) questioned the logical basis for this state of the law, asking, if the underlying principle of the confessions rule is that involuntary confessions are unreliable, and if such reasoning is valid, "how can it logically be said that confessions improperly extracted by persons not defined as 'persons in authority' are any more reliable than those extracted by persons in authority" (para. 21)? As Nowlin (2004) argues, surely the anticipation of professional advancement in a powerful and wealthy criminal organization falls within this framework, not to mention the assistance the organization is offering the target to circumvent an imminently devastating situation (conviction of a serious criminal offence). In addition, a target may fear reprisal from the criminal syndicate if he or she does not make the expected admissions.

Whereas the person in authority requirement is an integral part of the Canadian common law confessions rule, the problems associated with determining who is a person in authority do not exist in the United States because, as the Uniform Law Conference Report (1982) pointed out, the prosecution in the United States has to prove the voluntariness of all statements made by an accused person (cited in Brockman and Rose 2011: 221). Despite the English Criminal Law Revision Committee's recommendation to adopt a rule much like the one that exists in the U.S., both the Uniform Law Conference of Canada (1982) and the Law Reform Commission of Canada (1984a; 1984b) were opposed to such sweeping changes and advocated that Canadian criminal law retain the persons in authority requirement (cited in Brockman and Rose 2011: 221).

In *Hodgson* (1998), counsel for the accused asked the Supreme Court of Canada either to expand the scope of the common law confessions rule to include persons who are not persons in authority or to extend the scope of the definition of a person in authority so that all involuntary confessions are subject to the exclusionary rule, regardless of the recipient (See *Carter* 2001: para. 55).[8] Despite Mr. Justice Cory's recognition of the "very real possibility of a resulting miscarriage of justice and the fundamental unfairness of admitting statements coerced by the violence of private individuals," he remarked that such fundamental changes to the confessions rule "could bring about complex and unforeseeable consequences for the administration of justice" (*Hodgson* 1998: para. 29). In short, the Court declined to eliminate the requirement for a person in authority threshold determination, stating that such a sweeping change to the law "is the sort of change which should be studied by Parliament and remedied by enactment" (*Hodgson* 1998; also see *Grandinetti* 2005: para. 35).[9]

As alluded to, criminal organizations can be coercive and "are often held together with violence and ... the trust that is often associated with criminal organizations is based on a fear of reprisal for anyone who betrays the criminal organization" (*United States of America v. Burns* 1997: para. 4). Targets, by and large, argue that they provided undercover officers with inculpatory statements in order to placate members of the criminal organization they believe to be dangerous, to secure significant financial payouts, or perhaps both (*Carter* 2001: para. 27; *Fischer* 2005: para. 30; *Grandinetti* 2003: para. 46; *Hart* 2007: para. 63; *Holtam* 2002: para. 18; *Lowe* 2004: para. 233; *Skiffington* 2004: para. 12; *United States of America v. Burns* 1997: para. 4; *Terrico* 2005a: para. 2). However, since no clear or direct threats are made, a "Hodgson warning" in these circumstances is futile. Mme. Justice Smith's words in *Lowe* (2004), however, are representative of a warning the trial judge gave to the jury in these reasons for judgment: "Statements made in the course of an undercover operation must be viewed as inherently unreliable. It is dangerous to base a conviction upon such statements unless they are confirmed by independent evidence" (para. 370).

Indeed, to eliminate the person in authority requirement for the voluntary confessions rule would have far-reaching consequences for undercover police work. The Mr. Big strategy is no exception. Even though the accused would not subjectively perceive undercover police officers to be persons in authority, all statements stemming from an undercover operation would become subject to the confessions rule (*Hodgson* 1998: para. 25). Thus, in the context of Mr. Big, this post-offence undercover operation would, in all probability, cease to exist as an investigative technique.

In any event, Penney (2004) posits that Parliamentary intervention is not warranted in the circumstances because judges have the discretion at common law to exclude evidence where the prejudicial effect of such evidence outweighs any probative value it may have (295).[10] Penney (2004: 295) suggests the Courts could use this power to exclude statements that do not fall within the ambit of the common law confessions rule. However, as Chief Justice Scott observed in *Unger* (1993a), even though the trial judge has the discretion to "exclude evidence where the prejudicial value exceeds its probative weight, the ordinary rule is still toward an inclusionary policy" (para. 64). Penney (2004: 295) intuitively argues, that such "discretion should be exercised whenever there is a reasonable possibility that the trier of fact would give undue weight to a questionable confession." Although well intentioned, the common law discretion to exclude impugned confessions is arguably not an adequate safeguard since some judges may not be sufficiently mindful of the growing phenomenon of false confessions. Instead, Penney (2004: 296) puts forward for consideration the notion that the confessions rule should prohibit interrogation techniques that "experience and study have shown apt to produce false confessions."[11]

A General Exclusionary Rule

Despite the RCMP's claim that their technique "promotes candor and truth" (2009), Nowlin (2004) opines that the undercover elicitations are "of dubious reliability and have only the most tenuous probative value" (383). He argues that the Canadian criminal courts should seriously consider adopting a general exclusionary rule with respect to confessions obtained by virtue of Mr. Big undercover operations (383).

If Mr. Big confessions were excluded, the question would become, should any derivative evidence obtained from these inadmissible confessions be admitted as evidence at the accused's trial? For example, should the body of Bridges' victim (see Chapter 1), or the fact that Bridges showed the police the grave where the body of the deceased was found, be admissible? Applying the law as the Supreme Court of Canada outlined it in *Burlingham* (1995), this evidence would not be admitted, as the body would not have been found without the illegally obtained statement, and the fact that Bridges showed the police the grave site would be considered conscripted evidence (and therefore inadmissible). However, Justices McLachlin and Charron, for the majority in *Grant* (2009), recently revisited this interpretation of the *Charter* and rejected this "all-but-automatic exclusionary rule for non-discoverable conscriptive evidence" (para. 64). Treating conscriptive evidence as automatically unfair fails to consider "all the circumstances" as required under section 24(2) of the *Charter*. The two justices found that such an exclusionary rule is inconsistent with a fair trial, "one which satisfies the public interest in getting at the truth, while preserving basic procedural fairness to the accused" (para. 64). It is now unclear whether such evidence would be admissible using the *Grant* framework discussed earlier. It may be that the evidence of the body found in the grave would be admissible, and, perhaps, the fact Bridges showed them where the body was located inadmissible. Leaving the admissibility of derivative evidence to this late stage is probably an inefficient way of dealing with such evidence. There is also some question as to whether inadmissible confessions would be worth pursuing for these limited purposes. But perhaps the strongest arguments against allowing the admission of confessions and other evidence from Mr. Big investigations is the aspect of moral decay (discussed at the end of Chapter 4), — that is, the possibility of wrongful convictions and of a negative impact on due process as well as the integrity of the criminal justice system.

The Possibility of Wrongful Convictions

Wrongful convictions are an unfortunate but very real phenomenon in the Canadian criminal justice system. According to Ramsey and Frank (2007), wrongful convictions violate norms of individual justice, raise questions about public safety, and undermine public confidence in the administration of justice (437–38). For these reasons, they conclude, wrongful convictions "can damage the symbolic status of the criminal justice process.... This damage ultimately places a burden on the integrity, prestige, reputation, credibility, and effectiveness of the entire criminal justice process" (438). Thus, in order to prevent miscarriages of justice that may ensue, it is imperative that policies be implemented to minimize the likelihood of eliciting false confessional statements from the innocent. This goal may mean eliminating the Mr. Big investigative technique. An unfortunate corollary in the preservation of the integrity of criminal justice system is the reality that some perpetrators will not be apprehended. In *Mentuck* (2000b), Mr. Justice MacInnes expressed how tragic the death of fourteen-year-old Amanda Cook was, saying, "For her parents, family and friends, a conviction would end the resurrection of this sorrowful event brought about by trials and re-trials and would undoubtedly permit them to bring or begin to bring some closure to it" (para. 4). He did, nonetheless, acknowledge that equally tragic to the death of the victim in this case, "would be the wrongful conviction of one charged with her murder" (para. 5).

The U.B.C. Law Innocence Project, an initiative of the University of British Columbia's Faculty of Law, is currently conducting a review of twenty-three homicide convictions, of which the number resulting from Mr. Big investigations is unknown (Stueck 2009: 34). There have not yet been any confirmed wrongful convictions of justice resulting from a Mr. Big investigation. However, one might consider the tunnel vision that resulted in the undercover operation against Andrew Rose (featured in Chapter 1) as a miscarriage of justice.

The case of Kyle Wayne Unger also raises questions. The federal Minister of Justice and Attorney General of Canada, Rob Nicholson, ordered a new trial for Unger in March 2009, citing concerns that Unger may have been wrongfully convicted. The decision by the Crown not to proceed with a new trial and the decision by the trial judge to acquit Unger of all charges (Pritchard 2009) further suggest a wrongful conviction. A review of the case shows that a fairly compelling body of evidence substantiates this conclusion.

On the evening of June 23, 1990, Kyle Wayne Unger, then nineteen years of age, attended a rock music festival at a ski resort near Roseisle, Manitoba. The following day, the mutilated body of sixteen-year-old high school student Brigitte Grenier was discovered in a creek in a densely wooded part of the resort (*Unger* 1993a: para. 1). The co-accused, Timothy Houlahan, then aged seventeen, also attended the festival; however, the two accused attended the festival separately, with their respective friends. Subsequent to a massive police investigation, Unger and Houlahan were charged with the first-degree murder of Grenier.[12] Prior to the completion of his preliminary inquiry, the Crown stayed the charges (para. 16). The RCMP then decided to launch a Mr. Big undercover operation with Unger as the target. Over the course of twelve days (not lengthy in terms of a Mr. Big operation), undercover operatives would initiate contact with and befriend Unger, giving him the impression that he could become a member of the criminal organization (para. 21). He confessed to being criminally involved in Grenier's death Brigitte (para. 22).

The prosecution's case hinged on testimony from a jailhouse informant claiming that Unger confessed to killing Grenier, his confession to undercover police officers, and hair fibre evidence consistent with Unger found on the sweatshirt worn by the deceased (*Unger* 2005: para. 2). Unger and Houlahan were convicted by a jury and sentenced to life imprisonment without eligibility for parole for twenty-five years (para. 2).

While the Manitoba Court of Appeal agreed to hear Unger's case, the Court ultimately dismissed his appeal from conviction.[13] Unger's application for leave to appeal to the Supreme Court of Canada was dismissed without reasons (*Unger* 1993b). The story, however, does not end here. On the contrary, a break in Unger's case would come almost ten years later.

On April 23, 2003, the Deputy Minister of Justice and the Deputy Attorney General for the province of Manitoba, Bruce MacFarlane, announced the establishment of the Forensic Evidence Review Committee to review homicide cases "from the previous fifteen (15) years in Manitoba in which hair comparison evidence was relied upon to secure a conviction" (Manitoba Justice 2004: 3). Of the initial 175 cases reviewed, two satisfied the criteria for revaluation, one of them being the Kyle Unger case.[14] The forensic evidence review committee decided to perform mitochondrial DNA (mtDNA) analysis on the microscopic hair comparison evidence originally tendered at trial, as well as samples provided by the accused, to determine whether the accused could be excluded as a source of the DNA from the exhibits. An examination of the hair and blood samples of Unger showed many differences between the mtDNA profile and that of Unger and concluded that the hairs were not from Unger (Manitoba Justice 2004: 20).

Having exhausted all avenues of appeal, counsel for Unger, under the conviction review provisions of the *Criminal Code* (sections 696.1-696.6), applied to the Minister of Justice to review his conviction of first-degree murder. In November 2005, Mme. Justice Beard of the Manitoba Court of Queen's bench, released Unger from incarceration pending a ministerial review of his conviction for first-degree murder (*Unger* 2005). Mme. Justice Beard found several inconsistencies in Unger's confession to undercover police officers, which brought into question the trustworthiness, or reliability, of his assertions.[15] Unger not only disclosed specific descriptions that were inconsistent with the facts of the case, he also made assertions that were patently false (para. 18). As Mme. Justice Beard pointed out, "The difficulty with these details is that they were not true" (para. 19). In addition, there was evidence at trial from several of Unger's friends and from his mother that Unger was a "bullshitter" and had a propensity to tell stories (para. 21).

Significantly, Unger's confession was no longer supported by the two other pieces of evidence; the microscopic hair analysis excluded Unger as a suspect, and the confession to the jailhouse informant was ultimately discredited and withdrawn by the Crown (Makin 2009: A9). As Mme. Justice Beard noted,

> The only remaining evidence is the accused's confession to the undercover police, which is fraught with serious weaknesses and which the investigators have suggested should be assessed by an expert in false confessions. If that report concludes that the confession was false, there will be no evidence against Mr. Unger. (*Unger* 2005: para. 48).

Mme. Justice Beard also pointed out that the Criminal Conviction Review Group of the Department of Justice's had recommended that false confessions expert Dr. Gisli Gudjonsson review Unger's confession (*Unger* 2005: paras. 6, 48).

Mme. Justice Beard ordered the release of Kyle Unger pending ministerial review, citing "very serious concerns that the applicant may have been wrongfully convicted and, apart from this conviction, there is no reason to refuse to release Mr. Unger" (para. 51). Unger had been in prison for thirteen years.

On March 11, 2009, federal Minister of Justice and Attorney General of Canada Rob Nicholson ordered a new trial for Kyle Unger. His decision came after a review of the "Investigation Report" and advice of the Department's Criminal Conviction Review Group;[16] the submissions of Mr. Unger's counsel and of the Attorney General of Manitoba; and the recommendations of Mr. Bernard Grenier, the Minister's Special Advisor on the criminal conviction review process (Department of Justice 2009). In a written statement, Nicholson stated, "I am satisfied there is a reasonable basis to conclude that a miscarriage of justice likely occurred in Mr. Unger's 1992 conviction" (Hutchinson 2009: A1). The evidence must have been compelling because this was only the fourth time that a justice minister ordered a new trial and did not refer the matter to a provincial appellate court for hearing (Makin 2009: A9). James Lockyer, a lawyer with AIDWYC, said, "It's hard not to see it as a comment by Mr. Nicholson that this case, as presented to him, is so overwhelming that it wasn't necessary, desirable or appropriate for a court of appeal to look at it" (Makin 2009: A9).

Lockyer speculates that Unger was a victim of tunnel vision, stating, "the police formed a theory before they had evidence of it, and then made the facts fit into their theory" (Giroday 2009: A4). He went on to say that they "formed a theory early on that two people must have committed this crime, for no reason, but that was their theory. So they managed to find two people who committed it, when only one really did" (Giroday 2009: A4).[17] Manitoba's deputy minister of justice, Jeffrey Schnoor, said Crown counsel would meet with RCMP to review the Unger file. He also indicated that the decision to retry Kyle Unger "will be based on whether the Crown has a reasonable likelihood of conviction and whether it's in the public interest" (Giroday 2009: A4). As indicated earlier, the Crown decided not to proceed with another prosecution.

There have been other allegations of miscarriages of justice and false confessions arising out of Mr. Big investigations, although some are still in the appeal process. For example, lawyers, academics, and the news media have questioned the so-called confessions by Denis Cheeseman and Shawn Hennessey in what has come to be known as the "Mayerthorpe massacre" (Brockman 2010; Staples 2009b; AIDWYC 2009). Hennessey recently dropped his appeal from his guilty plea because "It's very hard to withdraw a plea," and he is now proceeding with only a sentence appeal (Staples 2010). As mentioned earlier, Patrick Fischer's mother has been questioning the conviction of her son, alleging that the undercover officers induced him to falsely confess to a murder <www.injusticebusters.com/06/Fischer, Patrick.shtml>. Others have appealed unsuccessfully or perhaps abandoned appeals for lack of money.

The conclusion of the Unger case and other cases that may have resulted in false confessions elicited through the use of Mr. Big investigative tactics could have potentially significant consequences that reverberate throughout the criminal justice system. The exoneration of Unger could mean the end of, or at least a serious reassessment of, Mr. Big undercover operations.

Conclusions

The purpose of this book was to focus an investigative eye on the Mr. Big undercover operation — to explain how it works and to consider some of the legal and moral issues that arise from its use. In our view, it is a tool that should be curtailed or discontinued. If we choose to coexist willingly with controversial undercover policing tactics to control crime, we must come to grips with both the intended and the unintended consequences of such tactics. It is possible that we have adopted a complacent, uncritical attitude, insensitive to the dangers that "literally and figuratively lurk beneath the surface" of undercover operations (Marx 1988: 206). In the words of Marx (1988), we must be cautious "not to adopt a cure that is worse than the disease. The morality of the means is as important as that of the ends" (222).

Despite the RCMP's enthusiasm for this investigative technique and their claim that it provides "an environment where suspects feel comfortable in disclosing certain past activities which they may not otherwise discuss [and that it] promotes candor and truth, even about conduct that could be characterized as both criminal and shameful" (RCMP 2009), evidence on how it really works paints a somewhat different picture. As the trial judge pointed out in *Cretney* (1999: para. 29), these scenarios do not involve "afternoon tea and contract bridge parties." Deception, coercion, inducements, derogatory comments about women and children, and brutal criminal activities are all part of the ploy to elicit confessions.

The RCMP has recently garnered support for the use of this investigative technique through a public opinion poll. In 2008, 47 percent of 500 people surveyed for the RCMP strongly approved of the Mr. Big technique and 34 percent approved of it somewhat. This approval rating was from a population in which only 41 percent knew that the technique was used. In addition, the question was devoid of context or any details about how Mr. Big is conducted. The relevant poll question described Mr. Big as a technique "in which police officers pretend to be an important crime boss in order to get suspected criminals to provide evidence in an investigation" (2008: 6). The question provides no information on what the respondents might have known about how Mr. Big is conducted. In what appears to be a move to test the waters for further expansion of Mr. Big investigations, the RCMP also asked the following question: "Would you support Canadian police officers 'going undercover' by pretending to be a criminal or someone else in order to gain evidence of a confession from a suspected criminal for any crime that affects the safety of individuals or the community, or only for very serious crimes such as murder, sex crimes, major robbery, drug trafficking, or crimes affecting children?" (2008: 7) This double barrelled, multi-levelled question looks to further expand and contribute to the Mr. Big creep referred to in Chapter 3 — a situation in which individuals who were not initial targets of Mr. Big investigations appear in court as witnesses and, in some cases, as accused.

There are many reasons to relegate the Mr. Big investigative technique to the archives. A world that encourages the police to cross the line into illegal activities can more readily result in noble cause corruption and in wrongful convictions. Research has shown that false confessions continue to occur with regular and disconcerting frequency, and that interrogation-induced false confessions are becoming one of the more salient causes of erroneous convictions. As Gohara (2006) opines, "The demonstrated correlation between police deception during interrogation and false confessions leading to wrongful convictions should inspire timely judicial and legislative reform" (840). Mr. Big provides targets with many incentives to lie about or exaggerate their involvement in crimes, whether they committed them or not.

Even judges are starting to make excuses for undercover investigators who engage in illegal activities, despite the Supreme Court of Canada's warning that such behaviour undermines the rule of law. Techniques such as Mr. Big undoubtedly challenge democratic ideals of civil liberties, lower adherence to procedural due process, and call into question police accountability (Marx 1988: 15; Pogrebin and Poole 1993: 384). The moral decay discussed in Chapter 4 should also be of concern to us. Can we afford to allow the police to employ these clandestine operational tactics that appear to violate due process concerns and could potentially elicit false confessions? In the end, perhaps Mr. Justice Dubuc was correct in 1901 when he condemned similar tactics as "vile," "base," and "contemptible" (*Todd*: paras. 3 and 8).

Notes

1. This quotation is taken from *Unger* (1993a: para. 69). With respect to the Mr. Big undercover operation, the Manitoba Court of Appeal stated, "Courts should not be setting public policy on the parameters of undercover operations." As Sherrin explains,

"the courts have never sought to establish a comprehensive set of rules to regulate police questioning" (2005: para. 23).

2. See Brockman and Rose (2011: 206) for other differences between judicial authorization for consent surveillance and judicial authorization for surveillance where neither party consents.

3. There were a number of other cases that referred to judicial authorization, but it was unclear which section was used to obtain it.

4. Section 184.2(3) of the *Criminal Code* sets out the requirements for obtaining an authorization under the consent provision.

5. The Supreme Court of Canada's decision in *J.-L.J.* (2000) addressed the admissibility of expert evidence involving novel science. In evaluating the soundness of a novel scientific theory, the Court delineated four factors that would determine its admissibility: (1) whether the theory or technique can be and has been tested; (2) whether the theory or technique has been subjected to peer review and publication; (3) the known or potential rate of error or the existence of standards; and, (4) whether the theory or technique used has been generally accepted (*J.-L.J.* 2000: para. 33).

6. Penney (2004) argues that the constitutional right to silence is not extended to non-detained suspects because "detention shifts the nature of the moral relationship between criminal suspects and the state" (327).

7. According to Penney (2004: 281), "jurists have long recognized, however, that voluntariness is an imperfect proxy for reliability."

8. Similar arguments were made in *Copeland* (1995), *Forknall* (2003), and *McCreery* (1998a).

9. The Supreme Court of Canada has sidestepped making sweeping changes to the law on numerous occasions, maintaining that such fundamental changes to the law are a matter of legislative reform. See the cases of *Bow Valley Husky (Bermuda) Ltd. v. Saint John Shipbuilding Ltd.* (1997); *Copeland* (1995); *Forknall* (2003), *McCreery* (1998); *Salituro* (1991); *Watkins v. Olafson* (1989); and *Winnipeg Child and Family Services (Northwest Area) v. G. (D.F.)* (1997).

10. As stated by the majority in *Hawkins* (1996, para. 83), "The trial judge, of course, continues to be vested with the residual discretion to exclude such statements where their probative value is outweighed by their risk of prejudice.".

11. See White's (1997) discussion concerning the prohibition of interrogation tactics that create a substantial risk of producing a false confession (139-140).

12. At the time of the Brigitte Genier's death, Timothy Houlahan was seventeen years of age. Although an adolescent, as defined by the *Youth Criminal Justice Act*, he was transferred to adult court, a decision that was upheld on appeal to both the Court of Queen's Bench and the Manitoba Court of Appeal (*Unger* 1993a: para. 15).

13. Houlahan's first-degree murder conviction, on the other hand, was overturned on appeal. The cumulative effect of several errors at trial provided "the basis for a determination that there was a miscarriage of justice" (para. 173). However, Houlahan committed suicide in 1994 while awaiting a new trial (*Unger* 2005: para. 3).

14. The other case is that of Robert Stewart Sanderson (*Sanderson* 1999a).

15. The Manitoba Court of Appeal had earlier observed that, in his discussions with undercover police officers about the murder of Brigitte Grenier, Unger "got a number of the details of the murder wrong, [although] the essential features of the murder as he described them continued to be consistent with the physical evidence" (*Unger* 1993a: para. 60). Despite the fact that some specific descriptions were inconsistent

and at times wrong, Chief Justice Scott was of the view that this was "not significant in the totality of his confessions" (para. 60). At the time, other compelling evidence corroborated the confession.

16. Hutchinson (2009) indicates that the federal Justice Department's Criminal Conviction Review Group relied on a report from false confessions expert Dr. Gisli Gudjonsson (A1). An *Access to Information* request for this report was rejected under section 19(1) of the *Act* (personal information) and under s. 21(1)(2) (advice or recommendations) (letter from Francine Farley, Access to Information and Privacy Office to Joan Brockman, December 14, 2009).

17. In addition to evidence collected at the murder scene excluding Unger as a suspect, witnesses testified seeing Unger hanging around a campfire, and that "he did not have any mud or dirt on his clothing, or scratches or bruises to his face" (Unger, 1993a, para. 6). Houlahan, on the other hand, was seen emerging from the densely wooded part of the resort covered in mud, had scratches on his face and blood on his chin (para. 7). Moreover, a forensic orthodontist testified that the bite marks found on the victim's breasts and arm could not have been made by Unger (para. 9). The co-accused, Houlahan, refused to provide police with teeth impressions (para. 128).

Appendix

List of Mr. Big Cases

R. v. Anderson, [2009] A.J. No. 176 (C.A.)

R. v. Aubee, [2002] S.J. No. 410 (Q.B.); [2006] S.J. No. 620 (Q.B.)

R. v. Bicknell, [2003] B.C.J. No. 2312 (S.C.)

R. v. Blac, [2006] B.C.J. No. 3521

R. v. Black, [2007] B.C.J. No. 1644 (S.C.)

R. v. Bonisteel, [2008] B.C.J. No. 1705 (C.A.)

R. v. Boudreau, [2009] N.S.J. No. 67 (S.C.)

R. v. Bridges, [2005a] M.J. No. 232 (Q.B.); [2005b] M.J. No. 536 (Q.B.); [2006] M.J. No. 428 (C.A.)

United States of America v. Burns, [1997] B.C.J. No. 1554 (C.A.); [2001] 1 S.C.R. 283

R. v. Carter, [2001] B.C.J. No. 1760

R. v. Casement, [2009] S.J. No. 201 (S.C.)

R. v. Caster, [1998] B.C.J. No. 3178 (S.C.); [2001] B.C.J. No. 2185 (C.A.); leave to appeal refused, [2002] S.C.C.A. No. 3

R. v. Ciancio, [2006] B.C.J. No. 2926 (S.C.); [2007] B.C.J. No. 1192

R. v. C.K.R.S., [2005] B.C.J. No. 2917 (S.C.)

R. v. Copeland, [1995] B.C.J. No. 2114 (Prov. Ct.); [1999] B.C.J. No. 2837 (C.A.); [2000] B.C.J. No. 601 (S.C.)

R. v. Crane Chief, [2002] A.J. No. 1706 (Q.B.)

R. v. Creek, [1998] B.C.J. No. 3189 (S.C.); [2000] B.C.J. No. 1932; [2001] B.C.J. No. 1162; leave to appeal refused, [2000] S.C.C.A. No. 566

R. v. Cretney, [1999] B.C.J. No. 2875 (S.C.)

Dix v. Canada, (Attorney General), [2001] A.J. No. 1273 (Q.B.); [2002] A.J. No. 784 (Q.B.)

R. v. Doyle, [2003] N.J. No. 45 (S.C.); [2004] N.J. No. 351 (C.A.)

R. v. Eggleston, [1997] B.C.J. No. 2948 (C.A.)

R. v. Ethier, [2004] B.C.J. No. 775 (S.C.)

R. v. Evans 1988 CarswellBC 788 (C.A.); [1991] 1 S.C.R. 869

R. v. Evans, [1996] B.C.J. No. 3141 (S.C.)

R. v. Ferber, [2000] A.J. No. 1405

R. v. Fischer, [2005a] B.C.J. No. 1042 (C.A.); leave to appeal refused, [2005b] S.C.C.A. No. 308

R. v. Fliss, [2000] B.C.J. No. 1126 (C.A.); [2002] 1 S.C.R. 535

R. v. Foreman, [2002] O.J. No. 4332 (C.A.)

R. v. Forknall, [2000] B.C.J. No. 2969 (S.C.); [2003a] B.C.J. No. 108 (C.A.); leave to appeal refused, [2003b] S.C.C.A. No. 466

R. v. French, [1997] B.C.J. No. 2515 (C.A.)

R. v. G.W.F., [2000a] B.C.J. No. 1062 (S.C.); [2000b] B.C.J. No. 1853 (S.C.); [2003a]
B.C.J. No. 1229 (C.A.); leave to appeal refused, [2003b] S.C.C.A. No. 277

R. v. Giroux, [2007] B.C.J. No. 2206 (C.A.)

R. v. Grandinetti, [2003] A.J. No. 1330 (C.A.); [2005] 1 S.C.R. 27

R. v. Griffin, [2001a] M.J. No. 92 (Q.B.); [2001b] M.J. No. 213 (C.A.); [2002]
M.J. No. 107

R. v. Hambleton, [2006] A.J. No. 1561 (Q.B.)

R. v. Hart, [2007] N.J. No. 237 (S.C.)

R. v. Hathway, [2007] S.J. No. 245 (Q.B.)

R. v. Hennessey, [2008a] A.J. No. 1514; [2008b] A.J. No. 1521; [2009] A.J. No. 82

R. v. Henry, [1999] B.C.J. No. 74 (C.A.); [2003] B.C.J. No. 2068 (C.A.); [2005]
3 S.C.R. 609

R. v. Holtam, [2002] B.C.J. No. 1164 (C.A.); leave to appeal refused, [2002]
S.C.C.A. No.10

R. v. Jacobson, [2004] O.J. No. 3946; [2004] O.J. No. 6020; [2004] O.J. No. 933

R. v. Joseph, [2000a] B.C.J. No. 2800 (S.C.); [2000b] B.C.J. No. 2850; [2003] B.C.J.
No. 1526 (C.A.)

R. c. Lepage, [2003] J.Q. No. 26 (S.C.); [2005a] J.Q. No 1606 (C.A.); [2005b]
J.Q. No 1607 (C.A.); [2008a] J.Q. No. 248; leave to appeal refused, [2008b],
S.C.C.A. No. 112

R. v. Lowe, [2004] B.C.J. No. 1702 (S.C.)

R. v. Lowe, [2009] B.C.J. No. 1470

R. v. Mack, [2007] A.J. No. 1551

R. v. Macki, [2001] B.C.J. No. 573 (S.C.); [2001] B.C.J. No. 574 (S.C.)

R. v. MacMillan, [2000a] B.C.J. No. 2907; [2000b] B.C.J. No. 2821; [2003a] B.C.J.
No. 3156 (S.C.); [2003b] B.C.J. No. 1479 (C.A.)

R. v. McCreery, [1996] B.C.J. No. 2405; [1998a] B.C.J. No. 1199; [1998b]
S.C.C.A.No. 253

R. v. McIntyre, [1993] N.B.J. No. 293 (C.A.); [1994] 2 S.C.R. 480

R. v. Mentuck, [2000a] M.J. No. 69 (Q.B.); [2000b] M.J. No. 447 (Q.B.); [2001]
3 S.C.R. 442

R. v. Moore, [1997] B.C.J. No. 1569 (C.A.)

R. v. Nette, [1998] B.C.J. No. 3243 (S.C.); [2001] 3 S.C.R.

R. v. O.N.E., [2000a] B.C.J. 1922 (S.C.); [2000b] B.C.J 1923 (S.C.) [2001] 3
S.C.R. 478

R. v. Osmar, [2001] O.J. No. 5797 (Gen. Div.); [2007a] O.J. No. 244 (C.A.); leave
to appeal refused, [2007b], No. 157

R. v. Parsons, [1996] N.J. No. 317

R. v. Perovic, [2004a] B.C.J. No. 3037 (S.C.); [2004b] B.C.J. No. 3058 (S.C.)

R. v. Peterffy, [2000] B.C.J. No. 338 (C.A.)

R. v. Porsch, [2007] B.C.J. No. 2393; [2008] B.C.J. No. 2553

R. v. Proulx, [2005] B.C.J. No. 272 (S.C.)

R. v. R.K.C., [2004] B.C.J. No. 554 (S.C.)

R. v. Raza, [1998] B.C.J. No. 3246 (S.C.)

R. v. Redd, [1999] B.C.J. No. 1471 (S.C.); [2002] B.C.J. No. 1104 (C.A.); leave to appeal refused, [2002] S.C.C.A. No. 315

R. v. Roberts, [1997] B.C.J. No. 765 (C.A.)

R. v. Roop, [2007] B.C.J. No. 3019 (S.C.)

R. v. Rose, [1991] B.C.J. No. 4026 (C.A.); [1992], B.C.J. No. 279 (C.A.); [1998] B.C.J. No. 1360

R. v. Sihota, [2009] B.C.J. No. 9 (S.C.)

R. v. Simmonds, [2000a] B.C.J. No. 1309 (S.C.); [2000b] B.C.J. No. 1316 (S.C.); [2002] B.C.J.No. 1132 (C.A.); leave to appeal refused, [2002] S.C.C.A No. 1314

R. v. Skiffington, [2004] B.C.J. No. 1045 (C.A.)

R. v. Skinner, [1992] M.J. No. 570 (Q.B.); [1993] M.J. No.640 (C.A.); leave to appeal refused, [1994] S.C.C.A. No. 81

R. v. Smith, [2003] B.C.J. No. 3286 (S.C.)

R. v. Steadman, [2007] B.C.J. No. 2989; [2008a] B.C.J. No. 2284; [2008b] B.C.J. No. 2420

R. v. Steele, [2006] B.C.J. No. 1590 (C.A.)

R. v. T.C.M., [2007] B.C.J. No. 2705 (S.C.)

R. v. Terrico, [2005a] B.C.J. No. 1452 (C.A.); leave to appeal to refused, [2005b] S.C.C.A. No. 413

R. v. Therrien, [2005] B.C.J. No. 897 (S.C.)

R. v. Therrien, [2006] B.C.J. No. 3146 (S.C.); [2006] B.C.J. No. 3156 (S.C.)

R. v. Turcotte, [2005] 2 S.C.R. 519.

R. v. Unger 1992 CarswellMan 336 (Q.B.); [1993a] M.J. No. 363 (C.A.); [1993b] S.C.C.A. No. 486

Unger v. Canada (Minister of Justice), [2005] M.J. No. 396 (Q.B.)

R. v. Valliere, [2004] B.C.J. No. 2822 (S.C.); 2005, B.C.J. No. 185 (S.C.)

R. v. Wilson, [2007] B.C.J. No. 2892 (S.C.)

R. v. Wytyshyn, [2002] A.J. No. 1389 (C.A.); leave to appeal refused, [2003] S.C.C.A. No. 218

References

AIDWYC. 2009. July 21. "Mr. Big Confessions about Mayerthorpe Massacre Not Reliable, Says Prof." <www.aidwyc.org/news/article.264896-Mr_Big_confessions_about_ Mayerthorpe_massacre_not_reliable_says_prof> accessed September 4, 2009.

Amir, M. 2003. "Criminal Undercover Agents or 'Bad People' Doing 'Good Things.'" *Substance Use and Misuse* 38: 1425–31.

Anderson, B., and D. Anderson. 2009. *Manufacturing Guilt: Wrongful Convictions in Canada.* Halifax: Fernwood Publishing.

Baron, E. 2008a. "Armed with Lies, They Hunt for the Truth: In an Unprecedented Move, the RCMP Shed Light on Their Successful but Controversial Undercover Operations." *The Province* November 2: A4.

_____. 2008b. "He's a Shape-Shifter: Undercover Cop Never Lets His Guard Down When Playing 'Mr. Big.'" *The Province* November 4: A8.

_____. 2008c. "Innocent? Or Guilty? Atif Rafay Told Undercover Cops He Killed His Parents and Sister to Become 'Richer and More Prosperous and More Successful.'" *The Province* November 5: A11.

_____. 2008d. "'Bottom Line Is Truth'; Proponents of 'Mr. Big' Stings Say the Controversial Technique Is Vital to Solving Hard-to-crack Murder Cases." *The Province* November 6: A10.

BBC News. 2008. "Man Admits Rachel Nickell Killing." *BBC News*, December 18. <http:// news.bbc.co.uk/2/hi/uk_news/england/london/7783796.stm> accessed July 10, 2009.

Beauchamp, J. 2009. Telephone conversation with Joan Brockman. August 26.

Bedau, H.A., and M.L. Radelet. 1987. "Miscarriages of Justice in Potentially Capital Cases." *Stanford Law Review* 40: 21–179.

Bedau, H.A., M.L. Radelet, and C.E. Putnam. 1992. *In Spite of Innocence: Erroneous Convictions in Capital Cases.* Boston: Northeastern University Press.

Bellemare, J., and R. Finlayson. 2004. *Report on the Prevention of Miscarriages of Justice.* Ottawa: Federal-Provincial Territorial Heads of Prosecutions Committee Working Group.

Bogard, W. 1996. *The Simulation of Surveillance: Hypercontrol in Telematic Societies.* Cambridge: Cambridge University Press.

Borchard, E. 1932. *Convicting the Innocent: Sixty-five Actual Errors of Criminal Justice.* New Haven, CT: Yale University Press.

Bornstein, B. 1999. "The Ecological Validity of Jury Simulations: Is the Jury Still Out?" *Law and Human Behavior* 23, 75–91.

Boyd, S.C., D.E. Chunn, and R. Menzies (eds.). 2002. *Toxic Criminology: Environment, Law and the State in Canada.* Halifax: Fernwood Publishing.

Brandon, R., and C. Davies. 1973. *Wrongful Imprisonment: Mistaken Convictions and their Consequences.* London, England: Allen and Unwin.

Brautigam, T. 2007a. "N.L. Man Found Guilty of Drowning Twin Three-Year-Old Girls" Final Edition. *Whitehorse Star*, March 28: 16.

_____. 2007b. "Fake Criminal Gang Used to Arrest Twins' Father." *The Globe and Mail* March 13: A8.

_____. 2007c. "Lawyers Question Ruse that Led to Conviction." *New Brunswick Telegraph Journal* April 2: A4.

Breau, D.L., and B. Brook. 2007. "'Mock' Mock Juries: A Field Experiment on the Ecological Validity of Jury Simulations." *Law and Psychology Review* 31: 77–92.

Brockman, J. 2010. "'An Offer You Can't Refuse': Pleading Guilty When Innocent." *Criminal Law Quarterly* 56 (1): 116–37.

Brockman, J., and D.E. Chunn. 1993. "Gender Bias in Law and the Social Sciences." In Joan Brockman and Dorothy. E. Chunn (eds.), *Investigating Gender Bias: Law, Courts and the Legal Profession.* Toronto: Thompson Educational Publishing.

Brockman, J., and V.G. Rose. 2011. *An Introduction to Canadian Criminal Procedure and Evidence.* Fourth edition. Scarborough, ON: Thomson Nelson.

Bronitt, S. 2004. "The Law in Undercover Policing: A Comparative Study of Entrapment and Covert Interviewing in Australia, Europe and Canada." *Common Law, World Review* 33: 35–80.

Burke, A.S. 2006. "Improving Prosecutorial Decision Making: Some Lessons of Cognitive Science." *William & Mary Law Review* 47: 1587–633.

Burke, T. (Director/Producer). 2009, January 21. "Someone Got Away With Murder." [Television Broadcast]. Toronto, ON: Canadian Broadcasting Corporation (CBC).

Burns, T. (Director/Producer). 2007. "Mr. Big: A Documentary." [Documentary]. Canada: Atlas Grove Entertainment.

Busby, K. 2000. "Third Party Records Cases since R. v. O'Connor." *Manitoba Law Journal* 27: 355–90.

Campbell, K.M., and M.S. Denov. 2004. "The Burden of Innocence: Coping with a Wrongful Imprisonment." *Canadian Journal of Criminology and Criminal Justice* 46: 139–63.

Cassell, P.G. 1996a. "All Benefits, No Costs: The Grand Illusion of Miranda's Defenders." *Northwestern University Law Review* 90: 1084–124.

_____. 1996b. "Miranda's Social Costs: An Empirical Reassessment." *Northwestern University Law Review* 90: 387–440.

_____. 1998. "Protecting the Innocent from False Confessions and Lost Confessions — and from Miranda." *Journal of Criminal Law & Criminology* 88: 497–556.

_____. 1999. "The Guilty and the 'Innocent': An Examination of Alleged Cases of Wrongful Conviction from False Confessions." *Harvard Journal of Law & Public Policy* 22: 523–90.

Cherry, P. 2005. "Trial Told How RCMP Created Fantasy World: Ruse Used to Trap Woman Accused in 1981 Murder." [All But Toronto Edition]. *National Post* February 25: A8.

Cheston, P., and J. Davenport. 2008. "Sex Killer Admits Manslaughter of Rachel Nickell." *London Evening Standard.* <http://www.thisislondon.co.uk/standard/article-23604409-details/Sex+killer+admits+manslaughter+of+Rachel+Nickell/article.do> accessed Retrieved July 10, 2009.

Conti, R.P. 1999. "The Psychology of False Confessions." *The Journal of Credibility Assessment and Witness Psychology* 2: 14–36.

Cooper, S. 2007. *Murder Conviction Appeal.* <www.northshoreoutlook.com> accessed August 30, 2007.

Cory, P. 2001. *The Inquiry Regarding Thomas Sophonow: The Investigation, Prosecution and Consideration of Entitlement to Compensation.* <http://www.gov.mb.ca/justice/publications/sophonow/toc.html> accessed February 11, 2009.

_____. 2004. August 19. "Forensic Evidence Review Committee: Final Report." <http://www.gov.mb.ca/justice/publications/forensic/index.html> accessed May 27, 2007.

Cutler, B.L., and D.M. Hughes. 2001. "Judging Jury Service: Results of the North Carolina Administrative Officer of the Courts Juror Survey." *Behavioral Sciences and the Law* 19: 305–20.

Dawson, F. 2008. "Meeting Mr. Big: Day 1." *The Province* November 2: A4.

Denov, M.S., and K.M. Campbell. 2005. "Criminal Injustice: Understanding the Causes, Effects, and Responses to Wrongful Conviction in Canada." *Journal of Contemporary Criminal Justice* 21: 224–49.

Department of Justice (Canada). 2009. March 11. "Minister of Justice Orders New Trial in Manitoba Murder Case." <www.justice.gc.ca/eng/news-nouv/nr-cp/2009/doc_32341.html> accessed March 11, 2009.

Deslauriers-Varin, N., P. Lussier, and M. St-Yves. 2009. "Confessing their Crime: Factors Influencing the Offender's Decision to Confess to the Police." *Justice Quarterly:* 1–33.

Doob, A., and H. Kirshenbaum. 1972. "Some Empirical Evidence on the Effect of s.12 of the Canada Evidence Act upon the Accused." *Criminal Law Quarterly* 15: 88–96.

Dorling, D. 2004. "Prime Suspect: Murder in Britain." In P. Hillyard, C. Pantazis, S. Tombs, and D. Gordon (eds.), *Beyond Criminology: Taking Harm Seriously.* London: Pluto Press and Black Point, N.S.: Fernwood Publishing.

Driver, E.D. 1968. "Confessions and the Social Psychology of Coercion." *Harvard Law Review* 82: 42–61.

Drizin, S.A., and B.A. Colgan. 2001. "Let the Cameras Roll: Mandatory Videotaping of Interrogations is the Solution to Illinois' Problem of False Confessions." *Loyola University of Chicago Law Journal* 32: 337–424.

Drizin, S.A., and R.A. Leo. 2004. "The Problem of False Confessions in the Post-DNA World." *North Carolina Law Review* 82: 891–1007.

Drizin, S.A., and G. Luloff. 2007. "Are Juvenile Courts a Breeding Ground for Wrongful Convictions?" *Northern Kentucky Law Review* 34: 257–322.

Dufraimont, L. 2008. "Regulating Unreliable Evidence: Can Evidence Rules Guide Juries and Prevent Wrongful Convictions?" *Queen's Law Journal* 33: 261–326.

Edwards, R., and G. Rayner. 2008. "Rachel Nickell: Sex Attacker Robert Napper Admits Wimbledon Killing." *Telegraph.co.uk.* December 18. <http://www.telegraph.co.uk/news/uknews/3830646/Rachel-Nickell-Sex-attacker-Robert-Napper-admits-Wimbledon-killing.html> accessed July 10, 2009.

Epp, J.A. 1997. "Penetrating Police Investigative Practice Post-Morin." *U.B.C. Law Review* 31: 95–126.

Everington, C., and S.M. Fullero. 1999. "Competence to Confess: Measuring Understanding and Suggestibility of Defendants with Mental Retardation." *Mental Retardation* 37: 212–20.

Feld, B.C. 2006. "Police Interrogation of Juveniles: An Empirical Study of Policy and Practice." *Journal of Criminal Law & Criminology* 97: 219–316.

Findley, K.A. 2008. "Can We Reduce the Amount of Wrongfully Convicted People without Acquitting Too Many Guilty? Toward a New Paradigm of Criminal Justice: How the Innocence Movement Merges Crime Control and Due Process." *Texas Tech Law Review* 41: 133–73.

Findley, K.A., and M.S. Scott. 2006. "The Multiple Dimensions of Tunnel Vision in Criminal Cases." *Wisconsin Law Review* 291–398.

Fischer, L. 2006. March 12. "Mr. Big Sting." <http://www.injusticebusters.com/06/Fischer,%20Patrick.shtml> accessed January 20, 2009.

Fitzgerald, O.E. 1990. *The Guilty Plea and Summary Justice: A Guide for Practitioners.* Toronto, ON: Carswell.

Fournier, S. 2009. "'Mr. Big' Tells How Pair Were Reeled In." *The Province* February 8: A9.

Frank, J., and B. Frank. 1957. *Not Guilty.* Garden City, NY: Doubleday.

Fraser, K. 2005. "Confessed Killer Sentenced to Life." [Final Edition]. *The Province* February 22: A8.

Gardner, E.S. 1952. *The Court of Last Resort.* New York: Sloane.

Garrett, B.L. 2008. "Judging Innocence." *Columbia Law Review* 108: 55–142.

_____. 2010. "The Substance of False Confessions." *Stanford Law Review* 62: 1051–19.

Giroday, G. 2009. "1992 Murder Conviction Overturned." *Winnipeg Free Press* March 12: A4.

Gohara, M.S. 2006. "A Lie for a Lie: False Confessions and the Case for Reconsidering the Legality of Deceptive Interrogation Techniques." *Fordham Urban Law Journal* 33: 791–842.

Gorbet, M.S. 2004. "Bill C-24's Police Immunity Provisions: Parliament's Unnecessary Legislative Response to Police Illegality in Undercover Operations." *Canadian Criminal Law Review* 9: 35–391.

Government of Newfoundland and Labrador. 1998. February 2. "Justice Minister Responds to New Evidence in Gregory Parsons Case." <http://www.releases.gov.nl.ca/releases/1998/just/0202n05.htm> accessed November 17, 2008.

Greene, E., and M. Dodge. 1995. "The Influence of Prior Record Evidence on Juror Decision Making." *Law and Human Behavior* 19: 67–78.

Gross, S.R. 1996. "The Risks of Death: Why Erroneous Convictions Are Common in Capital Cases." *Buffalo Law Review* 44: 469–500.

Gross, S., K. Jacoby, D. Matheson, N. Montgomery, and S. Patel. 2005. "Exonerations in the United States, 1989 through 2003." *Journal of Criminal Law & Criminology* 95: 523–53.

Gudjonsson, G.H. 1992. *The Psychology of Interrogations, Confessions and Testimony.* Chichester, England: John Wiley.

_____. 2003a. "Psychology Brings Justice: The Science of Forensic Psychology." *Criminal Behaviour and Mental Health* 13: 159–67.

_____. 2003b. *The Psychology of Interrogations and Confessions: A Handbook.* Chichester, England: John Wiley.

Gudjonsson, G.H., I.C.H. Clare, S. Rutter, and J. Pearse. 1993. "Persons at Risk During Interviews in Police Custody: The Identification of Vulnerabilities." *Royal Commission on Criminal Justice.* London: HMSO.

Gudjonsson, G.H., and N. Clark. 1986. "Suggestibility in Police Interrogation: A Social Psychological Model. *Social Behaviour* 1: 83–104.

Gudjonsson, G H., and L.A. Henry. 2003. "Child and Adult Witnesses with Learning Disabilities: The Importance of Suggestibility." *Legal and Criminological Psychology* 8: 241–52.

Gudjonsson, G.H., and H. Petursson. 1991. "Custodial Interrogation: Why Do Suspects Confess and How Does It Relate to Their Crime, Attitude and Personality?" *Personality and Individual Differences* 12: 295–306.

Gudjonsson, G.H., and J.F. Sigurdsson. 1999. "The Gudjonsson Confession Questionnaire-Revised (GCQ-R): Factor Structure and Its Relationship with Personality." *Personality and Individual Differences* 27: 953–68.

Hans, V., and A. Doob. 1976. "Section 12 of the Canada Evidence Act and the Deliberations of Simulated Juries." *Criminal Law Quarterly* 18: 235–53.

Harmon, T.R. 2001. "Predictors of Miscarriages of Justice in Capital Cases." *Justice Quarterly* 18: 949–68.

Hickman, T.A. 1989. *The Royal Commission on the Donald Marshall, Jr. Prosecution, Digest of Findings and Recommendations.* Halifax: Queen's Printer.

_____. 2004. "Wrongful Convictions and Commissions of Inquiry: A Commentary."

Canadian Journal of Criminology and Criminal Justice 46: 183–88.

Hunter, S. 2003. "Victim's Missing Fiancé Extradited from England." [Final Edition]. *The Province* June 25: A20.

Hutchinson, B. 2004. "RCMP Turns to 'Mr. Big' to Nab Criminals: Shootings, Assaults Staged in Elaborate Stings." *National Post* December 18: RB1.

_____. 2007. "Meet 'Mr. Big': A New Film Looks at an RCMP Method that British and American Police Aren't Allowed to Use." *National Post* August 18: A1.

_____. 2009. "New Trial Deals Hit to RCMP Stings: Man Nabbed in 1991 for Murder Using Decried 'Mr. Big' Tactic." *National Post* March 12: A1.

Inbau, F.E., J.E. Reid, and J.P. Buckley. 1986. *Criminal Interrogation and Confessions.* Third edition. Baltimore, MD: Williams and Wilkins.

Inbau, F.E., J.E. Reid, J.P. Buckley, and B.C. Jayne. 2001. *Criminal Interrogation and Confessions.* Fourth edition. Gaithersberg, MD: Aspen.

Jackson, J. 1992. "Juror Decision-Making and the Trial Process." In G. Davis and S. Lloyd-Bostock (eds.), *Psychology, Law, and Criminal Justice: International Developments in Research and Practice.* Oxford: deGuyter.

Jiwa, S. 2004. "Bellevue Police Letterhead Used by Undercover Police." [Final Edition]. *The Province* April 24: A24.

Johnson, G. 1997. "False Confessions and Fundamental Fairness: The Need for Electronic Recording of Custodial Interrogations." *Boston University Public Interest Law Journal* 6: 719–51.

Jones, C.S., and E. Myers. 1979. "Comprehension of Jury Instructions in a Simulated Canadian Court." In Law Reform Commission of Canada (eds.), *Studies on the Jury.* Ottawa: Law Reform Commission of Canada.

Joyce, G. 2008. "Statement of B.C. Man could be Unreliable"; Caption Only. [Photo: Canwest News Service / MASSIVE FIRE: Surrey...]. *Daily News* October 3: 10.

Kari, S. 2006. "Need to Catch a Bad Guy? Just Leave It to 'Mr. Big.'" *Globe and Mail* August 11: S1.

Kassin, S.M. 1997. "The Psychology of Confession Evidence." *American Psychologist* 52: 221–33.

_____. 2005. "On the Psychology of Confessions: Does Innocence *Put* Innocents at Risk?" *American Psychologist* 60: 215–28.

_____. 2008. "The Psychology of Confessions." *Annual Review of Law and Social Science* 4: 193–217.

Kassin, S.M., and G.H. Gudjonsson. 2004. "The Psychology of Confessions: A Review of the Literature and Issues." *Psychological Science in the Public Interest* 5: 33–67.

Kassin, S.M., and K. McNall. 1991. "Police Interrogations and Confessions: Communicating Promises and Threats by Pragmatic Implication." *Law and Human Behavior* 15: 233–51.

Kassin, S.M., and K. Neumann. 1997. "On the Power of Confession Evidence: An Experimental Test of the Fundamental Difference Hypothesis." *Law and Human Behavior* 21: 469–84.

Kassin, S.M., and H. Sukel. 1997. "Coerced Confessions and the Jury: An Experimental Test of the 'Harmless Error' Rule." *Law and Human Behavior* 21: 27–46.

Kassin, S.M., and L.S. Wrightsman. 1980. "Prior Confessions and Mock Juror Verdicts." *Journal of Applied Social Psychology* 10: 133–46.

_____. 1981. "Coerced Confessions, Judicial Instruction, and Mock Juror Verdicts." *Journal of Applied Social Psychology* 11: 489–506.

_____. 1985. "Confession Evidence." In S. Kassin and L. Wrightsman (eds.), *The Psychology* of Evidence and Trial Procedure. Beverly Hills, CA: Sage.

Kaufman, F. 1998. *Report of the Kaufman Commission on Proceedings Involving Guy Paul Morin*. Toronto: Ontario Ministry of the Attorney General.

Kennedy, L. 1986. "Foreword." In N. Fellows (ed.), *Killing Time*. Oxford: Lion Publishing.

Kerstholt, J.H., and A.R. Eikelboom. 2007. "Effects of Prior Interpretation on Situation Assessment in Crime Analysis." *Journal of Behavioral Decision Making* 20: 455–65.

Lamer, A. 2006. *The Lamer Commission of Inquiry Pertaining to: Ronald Dalton, Gregory Parsons and Randy Drunken: Report and Annexes*. Newfoundland and Labrador: Queen's Printer.

Law Reform Commission of Canada. 1984a. *Questioning Suspects*. Working Paper #32. Ottawa.

Law Reform Commission of Canada. 1984b. *Questioning Suspects*. Working Paper #23. Ottawa.

Leo, R.A. 1992. "From Coercion to Deception: The Changing Nature of Police Interrogation in America." *Crime, Law and Social Change* 18: 35–59.

_____. 1996a. "Inside the Interrogation Room." *Journal of Criminal Law & Criminology* 86: 266–303.

_____. 1996b. "Miranda's Revenge: Police Interrogation as a Confidence Game." *Law & Society Review* 30: 259–88.

_____. 1996c. "The Impact of *Miranda* Revisited." *Journal of Criminal Law & Criminology* 86: 621–92.

_____. 2005. "Rethinking the Study of Miscarriages of Justice: Developing a Criminology of Wrongful Conviction." *Journal of Contemporary Criminal Justice* 21: 201–23.

_____. 2007. "The Problem of False Confession in America." *Champion* 31: 30–34.

_____. 2008. *Police Interrogation and American Justice*. Cambridge: Harvard University Press.

_____. 2009. "False Confessions: Causes, Consequences and Implications." *The Journal of the American Academy of Psychiatry and the Law* 37: 332–43.

Leo, R.A., and D. Davis. 2009. "From False Confession to Wrongful Conviction: Seven Psychological Processes." *Journal of Psychiatry and Law*. <SSRN: http://ssrn.com/abstract=1328622>.

Leo, R.A., and J.B. Gould. 2009. "Studying Wrongful Convictions: Learning From Social Science." *Ohio State Journal of Criminal Law* 7: 7–30.

Leo, R.A., and R.J. Ofshe. 1998a. "The Consequences of False Confessions: Deprivations of Liberty and Miscarriages of Justice in the Age of Psychological Interrogation." *Journal of Criminal Law & Criminology* 88: 429–96.

_____. 1998b. "Using the Innocent to Scapegoat Miranda: Another Reply to Paul Cassell." *Journal of Criminal Law & Criminology* 88: 557–77.

_____. 2001. "The Truth about False Confessions and Advocacy Scholarship." *Criminal Law Bulletin* 37: 293–370.

LeSage, P.J., and M. Code. 2008. November. "Report of the Review of Large and Complex Criminal Case Procedures." <http://www.attorneygeneral.jus.gov.on.ca/english/about/pubs/lesage_code/lesage_code_report_en.pdf> accessed February 11, 2009.

Libin, K. 2009. "RCMP Used Strong-Arm Tactics." *National Post* January 21: A15.

Lions Gate Investigations Group. 2009. "Criticisms of the Mr. Big Technique in Homicide Investigations." Blog available at: <http://lionsgateinvestigations.com/lgigwordpress/archives/15> accessed February 17, 2010.

Loewy, A.H. 2007. "Systemic Changes That Could Reduce the Conviction of the Innocent."

Criminal Law Forum 18: 137–49.

MacAfee, M. 2005a. "Police Sting Coaxed Confession from Accused, Murder Trial Told." *Globe and Mail* June 15: A10.

_____. 2005b. "Murder with All the Grisly Details: Meticulous Answers Heard on Sting Tape Defendant Stunned as Arrest Is Made." [ONT Edition]. *Toronto Star* June 21: A12.

Macfarlane, B. 2006. "Convicting the Innocent: A Triple Failure of the Justice System." *Manitoba Law Journal* 31: 403–87.

MacFarlane, B.A. 2008. "Wrongful Convictions: The Effect of Tunnel Vision and Predisposing Circumstances in the Criminal Justice System." Prepared for the Goudge Inquiry. <www.goudgeinquiry.ca/> accessed February 14, 2010.

Maidment, M. 2009. *When Justice is a Game: Unravelling Wrongful Convictions in Canada.* Halifax: Fernwood Publishing.

Makin, K. 2000. "Gag Order Obscures Man's Innocence." *The Province* October 23: A3.

_____. 2009. "Justice Minister Orders Retrial in Sex-Slaying Case." *Globe and Mail* March 11: A9.

Martin, D. 2001. "The Police Role in Wrongful Convictions: An International Comparative Study." In S. Westervelt and J. Humphrey (eds.), *Wrongly Convicted: Perspectives on Failed Justice*. New Brunswick, NJ: Rutgers University Press.

Martin, D. 2002. "Lessons about Justice from the 'Laboratory' of Wrongful Convictions: Tunnel Vision, the Construction of Guilt and Informer Evidence." *University of Missouri-Kansas City Law Review* 70: 847–64.

Marx, G.T. 1988. *Undercover: Police Surveillance in America*. Los Angeles: University of Los Angeles Press.

Maxfield, M.G., and E.R. Babbie. 2008. *Research Methods for Criminal Justice and Criminology.* Fifth edition. Belmont, CA: Thomson Wadsworth.

McCormick, C.T. 1972. *Handbook of the Law of Evidence*. Second edition. St. Paul, MN: West.

McCulloch, S. 2008. "Jury Hears about Undercover Sting." *Cowichan Valley Citizen* May 9: 14.

McIntyre, M. 2006a. "Top Court Upholds Murder Conviction Enabled by Sting." *Winnipeg Free Press* October 7: A9.

_____. 2006b. *To the Grave: Inside a Spectacular RCMP Sting*. Winnipeg, MB: Great Plains Publications.

McMullan, J.L. 2005. *News, Truth and Crime: The Westray Disaster and Its Aftermath*. Halifax: Fernwood Publishing.

McMurtrie, J. 2005. "The Role of Social Sciences in Preventing Wrongful Conviction." *American Criminal Law Review* 42: 1271–87.

Medford, S., G.H. Gudjonsson, and J. Pearse. 2003. "The Efficacy of the Appropriate Adult Safeguard During Police Interviewing." *Legal and Criminological Psychology* 8: 253–66.

Meissner, C., and M.B. Russano. 2003. "The Psychology of Interrogations and False Confessions: Research and Recommendations." *Canadian Journal of Police and Security Services* 1: 53–64.

Melamed, K., & Anderson, S. (Producers/Directors). 2008, February 27. "Bad Day at Barrhead." [Television Broadcast]. Toronto, ON: Canadian Broadcasting Corporation (CBC).

Meyer, J.R., and N.D. Reppucci. 2007. "Police Practices and Perceptions Regarding Juvenile Interrogation and Interrogative Suggestibility." *Behavioral Sciences and the Law* 25: 757–80.

Moore, T.E., P. Copeland, and R.A. Schuller. 2009. "Deceit, Betrayal and the Search for

Truth: Legal and Psychological Perspectives on the 'Mr. Big' Strategy." *Criminal Law Quarterly* 55: 348–404.

Mossman, M.J. 1993. "Gender Bias in the Legal Profession: Challenges and Choices." In Joan Brockman and Dorothy. E. Chunn (eds.), *Investigating Gender Bias: Law, Courts and the Legal Profession*. Toronto: Thompson Educational Publishing.

Motto, C.J., and D.L. June. 2000. *Undercover*. Second edition. Boca Raton, FL: CRC Press.

Mulgrew, I. 2005. "So-Called 'Mr. Big' Confessions Bad Situation." *Vancouver Sun*. July 19: B1.

_____. 2007. "Maybe It's Time to Take a Close Look at 'Mr. Big': RCMP Ploy to Coax Confessions from Suspects Also Snares the Innocent and Can Leave Some Juries Confused." [Final Edition]. *Vancouver Sun*. September 3: B1.

Myers, D.G., and S.J. Spencer. 2001. *Social Psychology*. Canadian edition. Toronto, ON: McGraw-Hill Ryerson.

Nowlin, C. 2004. "Excluding the Post-Offence Undercover Operation from Evidence: 'Warts and All'." *Canadian Criminal Law Review* 8: 382–414.

_____. 2005. "Narrative Evidence: A Wolf in Sheep's Clothing, Part I." *Criminal Law Quarterly* 51: 238–64.

_____. 2006. "Narrative Evidence: A Wolf in Sheep's Clothing, Part II." *Criminal Law Quarterly* 51: 271–302.

Ofshe, R.J., and R.A. Leo. 1997a. "The Social Psychology of Police Interrogation: The Theory and Classification of True and False Confessions." *Studies in Law, Politics and Society* 16: 189–251.

_____. 1997b. "The Decision to Confess Falsely: Rational Choice and Irrational Action." *Denver University Law Review* 74: 979–1122.

Ogilvie, C. 1996. "Sting Details Come to Light: Judge Lifts Ban on Publication." [Final C Edition]. *The Province*. February 1: A5.

Ogloff, J.R.P., and V.G. Rose. 2005. "The Comprehension of Judicial Instructions." In N. Brewer and K.D. Williams (eds.), *Psychology and Law: An Empirical Perspective*. New York: Guilford Press.

Packer, H. L. 1964. "Two Models of the Criminal Process". *University of Pennsylvania Law Review* 113: 1–68.

Palmer, A. 2004. "Applying Swaffield: Covertly Obtained Statements and the Public Policy Discretion." *Criminal Law Journal* 28: 217–25.

_____. 2005. "Applying Swaffield Part II: Fake Gangs and Induced Confessions." *Criminal Law Journal* 29: 111–15.

_____. 2008. "Colin Stagg's Shadow Hangs over Undercover Police Work." *Telegraph.co.uk*. August 17. <http://www.telegraph.co.uk/comment/personal-view/3561512/Colin-Staggs-shadow-hangs-over-undercover-police-work.html> acessed July 10, 2009.

Palys, T. 2003. *Research Decisions: Quantitative and Qualitative Perspectives*. Third edition. Scarborough: Thomson Nelson.

Penney, S. 2004. "What's Wrong with Self-Incrimination? The Wayward Path of Self-Incrimination Law in the Post-Charter Era. Part II: Self-Incrimination in Police Investigations." *Criminal Law Quarterly* 48: 280–336.

Pogrebin, M.R., and E.D. Poole. 1993. "Vice Isn't Nice: A Look at the Effects of Working Undercover." *Journal of Criminal Justice* 21: 383–94.

Porter, L.E. 2009. "A Multivariate Model of Police Deviance: Examining the Nature of Corruption, Crime and Misconduct." *Policing & Society* 19: 79–99.

Powell, K., and C. Rusnell. 1999. "Project Kabaya: Mounties' Elaborate Ruse that

Fizzled; Thirteen-Month Undercover Operation Aimed at Dix Employed Wiretaps, Surveillance, a Staged Murder and 52 Police Officers — But Uncovered No Hard Evidence." [Final edition]. *Edmonton Journal* January 17: F1.

Pritchard, D. 2009. "Kyle Unger Acquitted of 1990 Killing." *Winnipeg Sun Online*, October 23. <www.winnipegsun.com/news/winnipeg/2009/10/23/11503791.html> accessed February 27, 2010.

Proquest. <http://www.proquest.com/en-US>.

Punch, M. 2000. "Police Corruption and Its Prevention." *European Journal on Criminal Policy and Research* 8: 301–324.

Radelet, M.L., H.A. Bedau, and C.E. Putman. 1992. *In Spite of Innocence: Erroneous Convictions in Capital Cases.* Boston, MA: Northeastern University Press.

Radin, E.D. 1964. *The Innocents.* New York: Morrow.

Ramsey, R.J., and J. Frank. 2007. "Wrongful Conviction: Perceptions of Criminal Justice Professionals Regarding the Frequency of Wrongful Conviction and the Extent of System Errors." *Crime & Delinquency* 53: 436–70.

RCMP. 2008. February. *British Columbia Attitudes Regarding Undercover Police Tactics: A Quantitative Analysis.* Vancouver: Drug Intelligence & Field Operations, RCMP E-Division Headquarters (acquired through an *Access to Information Request*).

_____. 2009. June 25. "Undercover Operations." <http://bc.rcmp.ca/ViewPage.action ?siteNodeId=154&languageId=1&contentId=6941> accessed September 2, 2009.

Redlich, A.D., and G.S. Goodman. 2003. "Taking Responsibility for an Act Not Committed: The Influence of Age and Suggestibility." *Law and Human Behavior* 27: 141–56.

Reifman, A., F.M. Gusick, and P.C. Ellsworth. 1992. "Real Jurors' Understanding of the Law in Real Cases." *Law and Human Behavior* 16: 539–54.

Roach, K. 1999. "Four Models of the Criminal Process." *Journal of Criminal Law and Criminology* 89: 671–716.

_____. 2007. "Unreliable Evidence and Wrongful Convictions: The Case for Excluding Tainted Identification Evidence and Jailhouse and Coerced Confessions." *Criminal Law Quarterly* 52: 210–36.

Rose, V.G. 2003. "Social Cognition and Section 12 of the Canada Evidence Act: Can Jurors 'Properly' Use Criminal Record Evidence." Doctoral Dissertation, Simon Fraser University.

Rose, V.G., and J.R.P. Ogloff. 2001. "Evaluating the Comprehensibility of Jury Instructions: A Method and an Example." *Law and Human Behavior* 25: 409–31.

Ross, J.E. 2008a. "Do Rules of Evidence Apply (Only) in the Courtroom? Deceptive Interrogation in the United States and Germany." *Oxford Journal of Legal Studies* 28: 443–74.

_____. 2008b. "Undercover Policing and the Shifting Terms of Scholarly Debate: The United States and Europe in Counterpoint." *Annual Review of Law and Social Science* 4: 239–73.

Russano, M., C. Meissner, F. Narchet, and S.M. Kassin. 2005. "Investigating True and False Confessions within a Novel Experimental Design." *Psychological Science* 16: 481–86.

Sangero, B. 2007. "Miranda Is Not Enough: A New Justification for Demanding "Strong Corroboration" to a Confession." *Cardozo Law Review* 28: 2791–828.

Saxton, B. 1998. "How Well do Jurors Understand Jury Instructions? A Field Test Using Real Juries and Real Trials in Wyoming." *Land and Water Law Review* 33: 59–189.

Scheck, B., P. Neufeld, and J. Dwyer. 2000. *Actual Innocence: Five Days to Execution and Other Dispatches from the Wrongfully Convicted.* New York: Doubleday.

Schehr, R.C., and J. Sears. 2005. "Innocence Commissions: Due Process Remedies and Protection for the Innocent." *Critical Criminology* 13: 181–209.

Sealy, A.P., and W.R. Cornish. 1973. "Juries and the Rules of Evidence." *Criminal Law Review:* 208–23.

Security Intelligence Review Committee. 2005. *Twenty Years of Independent External Review of Security Intelligence in Canada.* Ottawa: Cat. No. PS108-1/2005.

Severance, L.J., E. Greene, and E.F. Loftus. 1984. "Toward Criminal Jury Instructions That Jurors Can Understand." *Journal of Criminal Law & Criminology* 75: 198–223.

Severance, L.J., and E.F. Loftus. 1982. "Improving the Ability of Jurors to Comprehend and Apply Criminal Jury Instructions." *Law and Society Review* 17: 153–97.

_____. 1984. "Improving Criminal Justice: Making Jury Instructions Understandable for American Jurors." *International Review of Applied Psychology* 33: 97–119.

Seyd, J. 2007. "RCMP's 'Mr. Big' Stings Challenged; Documentary by Murderer's Sister Looks at Confessions." [Final Edition]. *North Shore News* August 24: 1.

Sherrin, C. 2005. "False Confessions and Admissions in Canadian Law." *Queen's Law Journal* 30: 601–59.

Siegel, A.M. 2005. "Moving Down the Wedge of Injustice: A Proposal for a Third Generation of Wrongful Conviction and Scholarship Advocacy." *American Criminal Law Review* 42: 1219–37.

Silbey, J. 2006. "Documentaries and the Law: Videotaped Confessions and the Genre of Documentary." *Fordham Intellectual Property, Media & Entertainment Law Journal* 16: 789–807.

Smith, S. M., V. Stinson, and M.W. Patry. 2009. "Using the 'Mr. Big' Technique to Elicit Confessions: Successful Innovation or Dangerous Development in the Canadian Legal System?" *Psychology, Public Policy, and Law* 15: 168–93.

Snider, L. 2000. "The Sociology of Corporate Crime: An Obituary (or: Whose Knowledge Claims have Legs?)." *Theoretical Criminology* 4: 169–206.

Sopinka, J., S.N. Lederman, and A.W. Bryant. 1999. *The Law of Evidence in Canada* Second edition. Toronto: Butterworths.

Soree, N. 2005. "When Innocent People Speak: False Confessions, Constitutional Safeguards, and the Role of Expert Testimony." *American Journal of Criminal Law* 32: 191–263.

Sorochan, D.J. 2008. "Why Do We Convict as Many Innocent People as We Do? Wrongful Convictions: Preventing Miscarriages of Justice Some Case Studies." *Texas Tech Law Review* 41: 93.

Staples, D. 2007. "Police Set Up Alleged Killers, Says Aunt: Family Suspects RCMP Used 'Mr. Big' Undercover Sting." [Final Edition]. *Calgary Herald* July 14: A13.

_____. 2009a. "Accomplice Admitted He Knew Roszko Would Kill Mounties: Confessed to Cop Posing as Underworld 'Mr. Big' during Elaborate Sting." *Edmonton Journal* January 29: A1.

_____. 2009b. "The Mystery of the Mayerthorpe Massacre: Part 31, The Final Chapter. Where We Explore What We Know and Don't Know about the Bloodiest Day in the Modern History of the RCMP." *Edmonton Journal* July 19. <www.edmontonjournal. com/news/mystery+Mayerthorpe+massacre/1806177/story.html> accessed September 4, 2009.

_____. 2010. "Hennessey No Longer Appealing Guilty Plea in RCMP Killings." *Edmonton Journal* online, January 21.

Stuart, D. 2001. "Oickle: The Supreme Court's Recipe for Coercive Interrogation." *Criminal*

Reports 36, 5: 188.

Stueck, W. 2008. "Man Guilty of Murder in Vancouver Blaze." *Globe and Mail* October 6: A3.

_____. 2009. "B.C. Law School Examining Potential Cases of Wrongful Conviction." *Daily Bulletin* January 23: 34.

Tataryn, L. 1979. *Dying for a Living: The Politics of Industrial Death*. Toronto, ON: Deneau and Greenberg.

Thurlow, M.D. 2005. "Lights, Camera, Action: Video Cameras as Tools of Justice." *The John Marshall Journal of Computer & Information Law* 23: 771–813.

Tibbetts, J. 2001. "Top Court to Rule on Police Secrecy: Newspapers Want to be Able to Report on Sting Tactics." [Final Edition]. *Ottawa Citizen* June 19: A3.

Tombs, S., and D. Whyte. 2003. "Scrutinizing the Powerful: Crime, Contemporary Political Economy, and Critical Social Research." In S. Tombs and D. Whyte (eds.), *Unmasking the Crimes of the Powerful: Scrutinizing States and Corporations*. New York: Peter Lang.

Trotter, G.T. 2004. "False Confessions and Wrongful Convictions." *Ottawa Law Review* 35: 179–210.

Uniform Law Conference of Canada. 1982. *Report of the Federal/Provincial Task Force on Uniform Rules of Evidence*. Toronto: Carswell.

Warden, R. 2003. "The Role of False Confessions in Illinois Wrongful Murder Convictions since 1970: Center on Wrongful Convictions Research Report." May 12. <http://www.law.northwestern.edu/depts/clinic/wrongful/FalseConfessions2.htm> accessed August 10, 2007.

White, K. 1990. "Confession Made to Bolster Reputation, Murder Trial Told." [4* Edition]. *Vancouver Sun*, December 6: A20.

White, W.S. 1997. "False Confessions and the Constitution: Safeguards Against Untrustworthy Confessions." *Harvard Civil Rights-Civil Liberties Law Review* 32: 105–57.

Wissler, R.L., P. Kuehn, and M.J. Saks. 2000. "Instructing Jurors on General Damages in Personal Injury Cases: Problems and Possibilities." *Psychology, Public Policy, and Law* 6: 712–42.

Wrightsman, L.S. 1991. *Psychology and the Legal System*. Second edition. Belmont, CA: Brooks/Cole.

Wrightsman, L.S., M.T. Nietzel, and W.H. Fortune. 1994. *Psychology and the Legal System*. Third edition. Pacific Grove, CA: Brooks/Cole.

Yan (second name not provided). 2009. "GA-3951-3-03400/09." Email to Joan Brockman. October 19.

Young, W., N. Cameron, and Y. Tinsley. 2001. *Juries in Criminal Trials, Report no. 69*. Wellington, New Zealand: New Zealand Law Commission.

List of Cases

R. v. Araujo, [2000] 2 S.C.R. 992.

Arizona v. Fulminante, 499 U.S. 279 (1991).

Beatty v. The King, [1944] S.C.R. 73.

R. v. B. (C.R.) [1990] 1 S.C.R. 717.

R. v. B. (F.F.) [1993] 1 S.C.R. 697.

R. v. B. (K.G.) [1993] 1 S.C.R. 740.

R. v. Beaulac, [1997] B.C.J. No. 2379 (BCCA).

Bow Valley Husky (Bermuda) Ltd. v. Saint John Shipbuilding Ltd. [1997] 3 S.C.R. 1210.

Brown v. Mississippi 297 U.S. 278 No. 301 (1936).

R. v. Bryce, [1992] 4 All ER 567, 95 Cr App Rep 320).

R. v. Burlingham, [1995] 2 S.C.R. 206.

R. v. Campbell, [1999] 1 S.C.R. 565.

R. v. Carter, [2001] B.C.J. No. 1760

R. v. Christou, [1992] 4 All ER 559, [1992] 3 WLR 228.

R. v. Collins, [1987] 1 S.C.R. 265.

Dagenais v. Canadian Broadcasting Corp., [1994] 3 S.C.R. 835.

R. v. Evans, [1993] 3 S.C.R. 653.

R. v. Foreman, [2002] O.J. No. 4332 (C.A.).

R. v. G. (S.G.) [1997] 2 S.C.R. 716.

R. v. Grant 2009 SCC 32.

R. v. Hawkins, [1996] 3 S.C.R. 1043.

R. v. Hebert, [1990] 2 S.C.R. 151.

R. v. Hodgson, [1998] 2 S.C.R. No. 66.

Ibrahim v. The King, [1914] A.C. 599

R. v. J.-L.J., [2000] 2 S.C.R. 600.

R. v. Khan, [1990] 2 S.C.R. 531.

R. v. Liew, [1999] 3 S.C.R. 227.

R. v. Mack, [1988] 2 S.C.R. 903.

R. v. Miller and Cockriell, [1975] B.C.J. No. 1040 (B.C.C.A.).

Miranda v. Arizona 384 U.S. 436 (1966).

R. v. Mohan (1994), 89 C.C.C. (3d) 402 (S.C.C.).

R. v. Mojtahedpour, [2001] B.C.J. No. 1238 (S.C.).

R. v. Oickle, [2000] 2 S.C.R. 3.

Prosko v. The King (1922), 63 S.C.R. 22.

R. v. Riley, [2001] B.C.J. No. 1618 (S.C.).

R. v. Rothman, [1981] 1 S.C.R. 640

R. v. Salituro, [1991] 3 S.C.R. 654.

R. v. Sanderson ,[1999a] M.J. No. 114; leave to appeal refused, [1999b] S.C.C.A. No. 275.

Sherman v. United States 356 US 369 (1958).

R. v. Singh, [2007] 3 S.C.R. 405.

R. v. Spencer, [2007] 1 S.C.R. 500.

R. v. Starr, [2000] 2 S.C.R. 144.

R. v. Stillman, [1997] 1 S.C.R. 607.

King v. Todd (1901) 4 C.C.C. 514 (Man. K.B.).

Tofilau et al. v. Queen, [2007] HCA 39.

Vetrovec v. the Queen, [1982] 1 S.C.R. 811.

R. v. W.(D.), [1991] 1 S.C.R. 742.

Watkins v. Olafson, [1989] 2 S.C.R. 750.

Winnipeg Child and Family Services (Northwest Area) v. G. (D.F.), [1997] 3 S.C.R. 925.

Legislation

Canadian Charter of Rights and Freedoms Schedule B to the *Canada Act 1982* (U.K.) 1982, c. 1

Criminal Code (R.S., 1985, c. C-46)

Mutual Legal Assistance in Criminal Matters Act (1985, c. 30 (4th Supp.))

Youth Criminal Justice Act (2002, c. 1)